SOCIAL SCIENCES DIVISION
CHICAGO PUBLIC LIBRARY
400 SOUTH STATE STREET
CHICAGO, IL 60605

THE CHICAGO PUBLIC LIBRARY

FORM 19

**NEW DIRECTIONS
FOR STUDENT
SERVICES**

Number 12 • 1980

NEW DIRECTIONS
FOR STUDENT
SERVICES

A Quarterly Sourcebook
Ursula Delworth and Gary R. Hanson, Editors-in-Chief

Number 12, 1980

Responding to Changes in Financial Aid Programs

Shirley F. Binder
Guest Editor

Jossey-Bass Inc., Publishers
San Francisco • Washington • London

RESPONDING TO CHANGES IN FINANCIAL AID PROGRAMS
New Directions for Student Services
Number 12, 1980
    Shirley F. Binder, Guest Editor

Copyright © 1980 by Jossey-Bass Inc., Publishers
    and
    Jossey-Bass Limited

Copyright under International, Pan American, and Universal Copyright Conventions. All rights reserved. No part of this issue may be reproduced in any form—except for brief quotation (not to exceed 500 words) in a review or professional work—without permission in writing from the publishers.

New Directions for Student Services (publication number 449-070) is published quarterly by Jossey-Bass Inc., Publishers. Subscriptions are available at the regular rate for institutions, libraries, and agencies of $30 for one year. Individuals may subscribe at the special professional rate of $18 for one year.

Correspondence:
Subscriptions, single-issue orders, change of address notices, undelivered copies, and other correspondence should be sent to *New Directions* Subscriptions, Jossey-Bass Inc., Publishers, 433 California Street, San Francisco, California 94104. Editorial correspondence should be sent to the Editors-in-Chief,

Ursula Delworth, University Counseling Service, Iowa Memorial Union, University of Iowa, Iowa City, Iowa 52242 or Gary R. Hanson, Office of the Dean of Students, Student Services Building, Room 101, University of Texas at Austin, Austin, Texas 78712.

Library of Congress Catalogue Card Number LC 79-92035
International Standard Serial Number ISSN 0164-7970
International Standard Book Number ISBN 87589-860-2

Cover design by Willi Baum
Manufactured in the United States of America

Contents

SOCIAL SCIENCES DIVISION
CHICAGO PUBLIC LIBRARY
400 SOUTH STATE STREET
CHICAGO, IL 60605

Editors' Notes — Shirley F. Binder — vii

Controls and Deficiency in the Policy Arena — A. Dallas Martin, Jr. — 1

What threatens American postsecondary education is not an overall federal policy towards such education but the continued legislative initiatives that enable individual federal agencies to establish specialized programs with no consideration for their total impact upon the educational institutions concerned.

The Allocation Process for Campus-Based Federal Student Aid Programs in the 1980s — Joe L. McCormick — 11

The new process for allocation of campus-based federal student aid programs is now two years old. Has it solved the problems associated with the old process?

The Handyperson's Guide to Student Aid Research — William D. Van Dusen — 25

Student aid research is not—or should not be—hard for the practitioner to do. Here are a few suggestions for why and how more aid administrators should add the term *researcher* to the list of their functions.

Student Consumer Information: The Right to Know—The Responsibility to Learn — Samuel Howell — 37

The choice of a college or university and a course of study is a significant decision for the prospective student. In a move to ensure the availability of adequate information on which to base that decision, the federal government has mandated that certain information be provided to all prospective students by institutions that receive federal Title IV financial assistance funds.

Peer Counseling: Can It Save Financial Aid Recipients on Scholastic Probation? — Jesús Gómez, Roberto Treviño-Martínez — 49

If professional financial aid counselors are not helping aid recipients to get off scholastic probation, perhaps they should step aside and let peer counselors show them how it can be done.

v

Computerized Operations in Student   Gordon E. Allen   69
Financial Aid: Relief or Restraint   James E. Zimmerman

A decision to computerize the student financial aid office requires careful consideration and systematic evaluation of need. Potential users must consider the trade-offs between unfamiliar technology, specialization, and inflexibility and speed, accuracy, and control in attaining organizational goals and operational objectives.

The Application of Open System   Shirley F. Binder   83
Theory to Student Financial Aid
Administration

The unprecedented growth and complexity of financial assistance programs have increased the necessity for administrators of college and university student financial aid offices to possess management skills so that those offices can be integrated into institutional plans and priorities.

Conclusion and Further Resources   Shirley F. Binder   95

Index   99

Editor's Notes

Student financial aid programs channel billions of dollars annually to students in postsecondary education. In addition to the support provided to individual students, the tuition dollars that these programs generate have become greatly significant to institutions facing real and projected enrollment decline and at the same time experiencing the impact of inflation on institutional budgets. Until 1976, scant attention was paid to fiscal aid programs either by the donor, the federal government, or by the institutions charged with administering the programs, but the following year saw both a noteworthy expansion in dollars allocated and students served and a tightening of the requirements for administration of the programs at the institutional level. Few decisions affecting financial assistance programs have been supported by research based on empirical data. Nevertheless, many decisions made in Congress and implemented through the regulatory process by the Office of Education have had a dramatic effect on students and institutions.

Chapters in this volume provide insight into the historical development of federal policy on the support of postsecondary education and on the development of the financial assistance programs that convey those funds to institutions through individual students. A model for research on the effects of student aid is proposed and programs designed to respond at the institutional level to changes brought about by legislation and regulation are described.

The first two chapters set the stage. In Chapter One, Dallas Martin places the federal policy on support of postsecondary education (if a policy can be said to exist) in historical perspective. He illustrates the fact that many decisions made in Congress and implemented through the regulatory process have not been based on research, and he points out the disastrous effect that well-intentioned decisions made without reference to empirical data can have and have had on students and institutions.

In Chapter Two, Joe McCormick summarizes the process by which campus-based federal financial assistance funds are allocated to institutions, describing the magnitude of the programs and the impact that changes in the process can have.

Not only has the major donor of financial assistance, the federal government, made decisions without reference to hard data but institutional aid administrators have not contributed significantly to knowledge about the effect of aid on students and institutions. In Chapter Three, Bill Van Dusen offers a conceptual framework for research that involves each of the partners—government, postsecondary institutions, private donors, agencies, and students—as researchers.

Provision of direct aid to students through the Basic Educational Opportunity Grant program in 1972 introduced students to their role as consumers. Since that time, laws and regulations have been written concerning the responsibilities of institutions to provide certain information to students. In Chapter Four, Sam Howell describes these responsibilities and proposes steps to be taken by an institution to implement a student consumer program and to comply with the spirit as well as the letter of the law.

Changes in regulations, liberalization of program eligibility requirements, and increases in available funds, enrollments, or both all result in pressure on an institution's financial aid staff. One resource that has not been fully utilized is student paraprofessionals. A model student counseling component that works with financial aid recipients who are experiencing academic difficulty is described by Jesús Gómez and Bob Treviño-Martínez in Chapter Five.

In the face of expanding financial assistance programs, tightened regulations, audits, and program reviews, institutions have looked to computer support for relief and assurance of data control. However, implementation of computer assistance without sufficient planning and without assurance of future maintenance of software programs can result in disappointment, an actual increase in man-hours required, work slowdowns up to and including sabotage in a desire to return to a manual system. In Chapter Six, Gordon Allen and Jim Zimmerman provide a guide for institutions considering mechanization of their financial aid system and a model for organizational support of system development.

In Chapter Seven, Shirley Binder addresses the need for increased emphasis on management skills among institutional administrators charged with responsibility for student assistance. A theoretical model for planning and improved integration of financial aid services into an institution's long-range plans and priorities is suggested. The role of the aid administrator as change agent on campus is pointed out, and alternative responses to dramatic changes in financial aid programs are identified.

It is hoped that this volume will provide administrators in higher education with insight into the problems faced by directors of student financial aid. This volume is also intended to provide institutional aid administrators and others with programs and strategies that may be useful in implementing changes required by changing federal laws and regulations. The general direction of the financial assistance programs has been ordained; that is, federal assistance to postsecondary education will be channelled to institutions through students. However, changes in the programs that serve as the vehicle for these funds can be expected to continue to occur. In order to maximize the planned effects of these programs — that is, to provide access, choice, and persistence to low- and middle-income students seeking postsecondary education — these changes must be met at the institutional level by well-managed and well-supported aid offices that have service to students as their main objective.

Shirley F. Binder
Guest Editor

Shirley F. Binder is director of student financial aid and assistant vice-president for student affairs at the University of Texas at Austin.

What threatens American postsecondary education is not an overall federal policy toward education but the continued legislative initiatives that enable individual federal agencies to establish specialized programs with no consideration for their total impact upon the educational institutions concerned.

Controls and Deficiency in the Policy Arena

A. Dallas Martin, Jr.

For years, scholars have examined factors which seemed to influence the formulation of federal educational policy in an attempt to thoroughly understand how that policy may be modified or expanded. National concerns for specialized manpower needs; inducements to expand research which in turn were expected to create new technological advancements that would lead to increased productivity; and attempts to minimize lost talent and reduce poverty have all been reasons that have been used to expand programs and to increase expenditures. While the general public has seemed to endorse these initiatives, some express concern over increased reliance upon such programs and the resulting impact and control that the federal government may come to exert upon America's postsecondary education system. Such fear is not new, however; it has existed since our country began.

Early Concerns over Federal Control

While education is not mentioned in the Constitution of the United States, there is strong evidence that, soon after the colonies were established, the importance of establishing and supporting an educational system in this new country was recognized. The Federation of Sovereign States, formed primarily to provide for the common defense, soon began to concern itself more with the general and social welfare of its citizens, and a part of this concern involved the educational needs of the people.

In 1787, two representatives at the Constitutional Convention proposed that the new government establish a series of federal institutions of higher education, but the idea was disapproved by the delegates as unnecessary. Nevertheless, that same body reaffirmed its support for education and adopted the Northwest Ordinance of 1787. This ordinance, which extended a similar enactment of 1785, required that the funds obtained from the sale of one section of every township were to be used for the support of public schools.

In spite of legislators' early actions to foster formal education, the omission of the term *education* from the Constitution is responsible for many hours of emotional debate among proponents and opponents of federal aid to education.

To justify their position, proponents of federal support usually cite the "general welfare clause" of the Constitution, contained in Article II, Section 8, which states that "The Congress shall have power to lay and collect taxes, duties, imports, and excises, to pay the debts and provide for the common defense and general welfare of the United States . . ,". Opponents of such support justify their opposition by the tenth amendment, which states that "The powers not delegated to the United States by the Constitution, nor prohibited by it to the States, are reserved to the States respectively, or to the people."

In spite of these two conflicting interpretations of the Constitution, historical events would seem to suggest that federal involvement in education is not unconstitutional. Still, some Americans are alarmed by proposals that seem to diminish state and local control over education.

Actually, there is little evidence of undue overt control of education by the federal government either in the past or at present. The alleged threat of federal control has often been used as a screen by those who oppose federal assistance on other grounds.

However, state "control" of education has increased in the past twenty years—a phenomenon that has both its virtues and its defects. One example of state involvement can be seen in the attempts to equalize education through consolidation of local school districts. Nevertheless, what is necessary and desirable for elementary and secondary schools may be a potential danger to public institutions of higher education.

State institutions, no less than private institutions, require freedom for research, investigation, teaching, and self-direction if they are to remain true learning institutions. However, some recent events and decisions regarding higher education, which affect both public and private institutions, indicate that the institutional autonomy which is absolutely essential is not very firmly established. Decisions to limit enrollment, reappropriate external funds, and restrict certain areas of research seem to suggest that most of the self-conscious governmental control of higher education will come from state and local government.

As for federal control of higher education, there is little evidence either of direct controls by the federal government or its agencies over public and private higher education or of the desire for such controls. However, as Richard Axt (1952, p. 14) suggests, the programs and policies of higher education are influenced by the many separate, uncoordinated federal programs in higher education, each of which emphasizes the interest of the federal department or agency that sponsors it rather than the general needs of higher education.

Growth in Specialized Federal Programs

This often unnoticed kind of control becomes apparent when the specialized nature of present federal programs is reviewed. It cannot be said too often that what threatens American postsecondary education is not an overall federal policy towards education but the continued legislative initiatives that enable individual federal agencies to establish specialized programs with no consideration for their total impact upon the educational institutions concerned.

This threat becomes still more evident when the numerous federal education activities are inventoried. To suggest the wide scope of federal interests, one needs only to mention aid to strengthen developing institutions; the GI Bill of Rights; military, naval, coast guard, and air academies; educational information centers; foreign studies and language development; land-grant colleges; the Library of Congress; low postal rates for books and periodicals; cooperative education, consumer education; teacher centers; veteran's cost of instruction; law school clinical experience, mining fellowships; basic grants; educational policy research centers; law enforcement education programs; occupational safety and health training grants; state student incentive grants; nurse practitioners training programs; schools of public health; vocational rehabilitation training; international educational centers; college work study programs; schools for Indians; the Job Corps; and the State Department's Educational Exchange Program.

Nevertheless, as Sidney Tiedt (1966, p. 3) has noted, few Americans would deny increased federal assistance for education. It is clear that the United States could never have assumed the position of world leadership which it presently holds without a highly developed educational system. Our leaders have repeatedly stressed the vital nature of education. As Thomas Jefferson, one of the great spokesmen for education, put it, in notes on the state of Virginia,"The commonwealth required the education of her people as the safeguard of order and liberty." One hundred and sixty years later, in his 1965 State of the Union message, President Lyndon B. Johnson indicated that one goal of his administration was to improve the quality of life in America and that education was an important component in such an overall plan. He went on to state that "higher education is no longer a luxury but a necessity."

In November of that year, his belief in and support for that goal culminated in the enactment of the Higher Education Act of 1965, an omnibus measure which broadened the nation's commitment to higher education and opened the door to thousands of students who had not been served. This expansion of educational opportunity continues to further public support for education, and it has also encouraged our law makers to endorse additional programs and increased expenditures. In addition, many more citizens have taken advantage of America's postsecondary educational opportunities. American higher education is no longer the birthright of the elite and the well-to-do; rather, it has grown to an enterprise which serves more than twelve million students. However, the immensity and complexity of our current system of postsecondary education has not silenced the critics who berate it as inefficient and unnecessary. In addition, the increase in the number and size of programs has made it difficult for supporters to demonstrate both their beneficial impact upon society and the worth of the public's investment in its citizens. While the debate will undoubtedly continue, one thing is clear— federal assistance has increased significantly during the last two decades, primarily as a result of the growth in student aid programs. In testimony before the Subcommittee on Postsecondary Education of the House Committee on Education and Labor, Michael O'Keefe (1979) indicated that the total federal allotment to postsecondary education increased from

$2 billion in 1965 to $13 billion in 1979. While the total increase represents an annual increase of approximately 13 percent, it should be noted that federal outlays for student aid, which comprised about $200 million in 1965, reached almost $8 billion in 1979—an average rate of increase of 30 percent per year.

In the face of such rapid increase, institutions of postsecondary education are still endeavoring to develop administrative policies and procedures that can handle this sudden growth and distribute financial assistance to students on a large scale.

A few decades ago, when colleges were small and available funds were more modest, systems for granting student aid were casual. Deans, departments, and professors made awards on the basis of subjective evaluation of student candidates. Administration was leisurely, and coordination of awards was effected informally. However, as institutions and programs have grown, the informality and intimacy have been reduced.

Rising program operations and increased living expenses forced the cost of college attendance dramatically upward. Those who in earlier years would have been able to meet the modest costs of college must now be considered just as needy as the students who would have needed such assistance in the past.

The same factors that have caused Americans to be concerned about the position of the nation as the leader of the free world have made them increasingly aware of the loss of able manpower from our educational system. The fact that many of our ablest citizens are unable to obtain a postsecondary education has made many Americans aware of the financial obstacles that stand in the way. This recognition may have been one of the primary factors that led Congress to pass the Middle Income Student Assistance Act of 1978. Previously, the emphasis of the federal government in postsecondary education had been to provide students from low- and moderate-income families with sufficient aid to obtain equality of educational opportunity. By the mid-1970s, concern was also being voiced about the plight of students from middle-income families, who are being squeezed out of postsecondary education by the increasing costs of attendance. While the evidence of a true middle-income financial squeeze was conflicting, it was inevitable that this problem would become a national concern. Likewise, it seems inevitable that many other problems will also become national concerns, and that this will bring the federal government into the educational scene as it has in the past.

Changing Federal Policy

However, there also are indications that the federal government has attempted to make its focus less specific than it has on past occasions. Many commentators have noted that the federal government's activities in postsecondary education have resulted in specialized programs that were enacted without regard to an overall educational policy.

As already indicated, however, the shift of federal support towards broad-based student assistance programs and the reduction in outlays for specific categorized programs would seem to suggest that federal lawmakers have attempted to pull back from the specialized programs and to provide an adequate base of balanced student assistance that can serve all citizens and all sectors of postsecondary education. All major higher education legislation approved since 1972 has placed primary emphasis upon the expansion and refinement of student financial aid programs. Nevertheless, these efforts have been partially thwarted by special interests, the lack of an adequate base of empirical data, and haphazard evaluation activities. These factors are not new, but they still create most of the problems and limit the effectiveness of legislators who are trying to arrive at reasonable solutions to current problems.

Informational Needs

In his book dealing with administrative behavior in the decision-making processes, Herbert Simon (1965, p. 58) noted that, "Since the legislative body must of necessity make many factual judgments, it must have ready access to information and advice. However, this must take the form not merely of recommendations for action but of factual information on the objective consequences of the alternatives that are before the legislative body."

It is unfortunate that, all too often, such information is not available. On several occasions in the past two years, members of the House Subcommittee on Postsecondary Education have asked representatives from the Office of Education (OE) to provide data on the income characteristics of participants in the National Direct Student Loan program. Repeatedly, OE officials have indicated that this information is not readily available. The lack of factual empirical data restricts the abilities of the members of Congress to make absolute judgments, forcing them to rely instead upon the advice and testimony of diverse and sometimes opposed interest groups. Such impediments to the decision-making process would be understandable, and perhaps even excusable, were it not for the fact that institutions participating in the National Direct Student Loan program have been required to provide detailed data to the Office of Education in their annual fiscal operation reports for the past twenty-two years.

Whether the existence of such a data base would have altered the legislative enactments that the Committee has supported cannot be known. Nevertheless, it is clear that the lack of such data is unfortunate.

Evaluation Results

Still another factor which often influences public policy decisions is evaluation activities. Each year, federal agencies initiate numerous evaluative studies designed to assess the effectiveness of current programs and administrative procedures. While these studies are valuable and produce important results, many of them have been awarded to contractors unfamiliar with the workings of the programs and many have been improperly conducted and completed in an untimely manner. Recently, the results of a quality control study prepared for the Bureau of Student Financial Assistance's Division of Quality Assurance by two outside consulting firms were reported in one of Washington's leading newspapers. The study, which had yet to be released by HEW, concluded that many errors in OE's largest student aid program were the result of complicated bureaucratic procedures rather than intentional fraud and abuse on the part of students and institutions. The study, which was later represented by OE officials as being substantially accurate, cost approximately $1.2 million dollars. Still, it is interesting to note that in responding to the report, OE personnel admitted that most of the recommendations made by the contractors had already been incorporated into program regulations and, although OE personnel admitted that they had no empirical evidence to this effect, they added that these changes seemed to be improving the overall administration of the program. Later, in responding to congressional personnel who had secured the report, OE officials admitted that the studies' sampling techniques gave their results insufficient statistical confidence to enable them to make corrective management responses and to determine reasons for certain errors. They also admitted that considerable caution had to be exercised when reviewing the dollar implications attributed to the errors and that the study had been begun before the Bureau of Student Financial Assistance had issued final preaward validation requirements designed to reduce such errors. Though such a study could have had real merit, it is clear that the absence of supervision regarding its design, timing, and release did not serve the information needs of public policymakers. In fact, the lack of control and coordination probably contributed negatively to the aid program being examined. The two examples of inappropriate responses by government agency personnel already cited should not be judged as the only contribution which agencies have made to the facilitation of public policy decisions. On the contrary, many positive actions and worthwhile studies have been initiated by governmental agencies. Recent modifications in regulations governing the criteria to be used in establishing fair and equitable institutional refund policies provide a clear example of how federal agency personnel, working in cooperation with representatives of higher education associations, can help to restrict creeping federal control, guarantee institutional autonomy, and still respond to congressional intent by correcting what Congress views as unnecessary practices on the part of a few institutions.

Special Interest Groups

Another factor which contributes to public policy making and the resulting political strategy is the special interests of organized groups. As Gladieux and Wolanin (1976, p. 253) have pointed out, higher education associations have existed for more than half a century, but the last twenty years have seen rapidly growing numbers of specialized associations and the establishment of Washington offices by universities and university systems. These organized special interests often work cooperatively to achieve specific policy goals. However, individual differences and competing priorities can also cause such groups to engage in competitive lobbying, which tends to be counterproductive and creates conflicting advice and information. This, in turn, forces lawmakers to choose among the various alternatives or to decide to refrain from making legislative changes at all. For these reasons, congressional personnel often have encouraged the representatives of higher education to resolve their differences and to arrive at a compromise position before advancing their recommendations.

The activities of these special interest groups and the ongoing evaluation studies by governmental agencies and external contractors provide a basis for the opinions that many legislators form of the need for public policy improvements. However, because the base of empirical data is often inadequate, members of Congress have increasingly relied upon their staffs to assist them in the law-making process. The final decisions rest with the members themselves, since they are elected to represent the people.

Services have been established to assist the members. The Congressional Research Service of the Library of Congress maintains its own data and will, upon request, provide any member with factual information and arguments for and against any position. Likewise, the Congressional Budget Office works with Congress to analyze and prepare budget requests, while the General Accounting Office prepares nonpartisan analysis and audits of how federal funds are administered. All these sources assist members of Congress in making informed public policy decisions. Still, perhaps the most important input which a member receives is direct feedback from his constituency and the recipients of the funds.

Conclusion

While the merits of federal support to postsecondary education will continue to be debated by purists of each camp, it is fairly certain that Congress will continue to support current educational policy directions that provide direct financial support to individual students.

The long-range effects of the policy may not be known for several years, but it already appears that educational opportunity has been greatly expanded to include a broader cross section of our society in our educational institutions. Also, the current direction seems to be well-accepted by the citizenry, and it has not diminished the pluralistic nature of our postsecondary educational system. Many educational administrators, however, are just beginning to recognize the impact that these decisions have had upon their institutions and to realize that their primary source of federal funding is the student aid programs. Consequently, they feel a need for redirection of institutional priorities, evaluation of existing aid policies, response to and compliance with student assistance regulations as they are adopted, and ongoing related research and evaluation. Such efforts will provide institutional spokesmen with the knowledge and data they need to assist and influence the policy decisions that are made in the political arena.

It may be hoped that by the end of the decade, such effort will also help lead us to a more economically stable and direct method of financial support for postsecondary educational institutions and for all our citizens.

While there is much to be said for the current diversified system of student assistance, it is also clear that this system is a complicated patchwork of programs with too many regulations and requirements. If America hopes to have a strong educational system that can provide for and serve the diverse needs of all its citizens, that system must be financed in large part by a direct price support system that encourages diversity and autonomy with minimal control.

References

Axt, R. G. *The Federal Government and Financing Higher Education.* New York: Columbia University Press, 1952.
Brockett, D. "Errors Mark U.S. Student Aid Program." *The Washington Star,* December 13, 1979.
Gladieux, L. E., and Wolanin, T. R. *Congress and the Colleges.* Lexington, Mass.: Heath 1976.
O'Keefe, M. Testimony of the Department of Health, Education, and Welfare before the Subcommittee on Postsecondary Education of the House Committee on Education and Labor. Washington, D.C., May 3, 1979.
Simon, H. A. *Administrative Behavior: A Study of Decision-Making Processes in Administration Organization.* New York: Free Press, 1965.
Tiedt, S. W. *The Role of the Federal Government in Education.* New York: Oxford University Press, 1966.

A. Dallas Martin, Jr., is executive director of the National Association of Student Financial Aid Administrators, Washington, D.C., and former director of program planning and administration of student assistance programs at the American College Testing Program.

The new process for allocation of campus-based federal student aid programs is now two years old. Has it solved the problems associated with the old process?

The Allocation Process for Campus-Based Federal Student Aid Programs in the 1980s

Joe L. McCormick

When President Harry S Truman appointed Earl McGrath as Commissioner of Education, he gave him this challenge: "Mr. Commissioner, I never went to college. I want every boy and girl in this country to go just as far with his education as his abilities and desires will take him. That is and will continue to be the educational policy of my administration" (Conrad and Cosand, 1976, p. 1). This marked a turning point in federal policy toward support for higher education. Every president since Truman has affirmed a national policy of providing students with both access to and reasonable choice among a wide diversity of postsecondary educational institutions. This national policy is firmly established in the over $6 billion dollars of federal student financial aid now available.

The purpose of this chapter is to examine the allocation process for the National Direct Student Loan (NDSL) program, the Supplemental Educational Opportunity Grant (SEOG) program, and the College Work-Study (CWS) program. These three federal student programs are commonly termed *campus-based* programs because these funds are allocated to postsecondary institutions whose responsibility it is to allocate the funds to the eligible students on their campuses. With the inflation, cutbacks in federal spending, and declining enrollments that postsecondary institutions will face in the 1980s, the methodology for the allocation of campus-based federal student aid programs has become more important both to the federal government and to the institutions.

Attention to the manner in which campus-based federal student aid funds were allocated to participating institutions was drawn by a report in 1974 from the General Accounting Office (Huff, 1979). This report concluded that the application process for campus-based funds was "subject to abuse" and "apparently not equitable." The GAO assessment that there were serious problems with figures in the applications was based on the finding that most institutions which it had reviewed had "inflated" their applications to qualify for higher funding levels. The GAO report recommended that future funding levels be based primarily upon historical, auditable data.

In 1976, the Secretary of Health, Education, and Welfare ordered the establishment of a study group to suggest inprovements in the management and operation of federal student financial aid programs. The study group's work was aided by seven well-attended public hearings held around the country. At these hearings, testimony was received from representatives of national and state associations, central and regional Office of Education staffs, student financial aid administrators, officials of state agencies, congressional aides, and others. One recurrent theme at these hearings was the need for changing the institutional application process for campus-based funds. Faults of the process then in effect were outlined in the study groups' report:

- The application was difficult and time consuming to complete, edit, and evaluate.
- The application encouraged grantsmanship.
- The application speculated on the future in that funding decisions were based on projections that were difficult to estimate and impossible to validate until two years had elapsed.
- Institutions reported that they were spending an inordinate amount of time gathering and verifying the data.
- The workload of applications and appeals that had to be processed varied widely from region to region, and this variation tended to foster inequities.

- The objectivity of the panelists was affected by the fact that the state allotment formulas caused schools in some states to receive less funding than the panel had recommended, while schools in other states received more than the panel had recommended.

The members of the study group agreed that the strengths of the application process were outweighed by its weaknesses and recommended the development of an alternative method of distributing campus-based funds.

Following the recommendations of this study group, the U.S. Commissioner of Education convened a panel of experts composed of financial aid administrators and other educators to review the campus-based allocation process. Chaired by Dr. Robert Huff of Stanford University, the panel of experts was given two primary responsibilities: to design a new process for delivering funds to individual institutions and make recommendations on the application process and the regional review process and to examine the state allocation formulas used to distribute funds to states and make recommendations for their modification or elimination. The panel of experts submitted its final report and recommendations to the U.S. Office of Education in June 1979. The new process for the allocation of campus-based funds adopted by USOE for 1979–80 and 1980–81 was derived primarily from the work of the panel of experts.

The Old Method of Allocation

Before one can understand the new allocation process for campus-based student aid programs, one must know something about the old method of allocation.

The initial phase of the allocation process began each year in October when postsecondary institutions filed a tripart application for federal student aid programs with the appropriate regional USOE office. This single tripart application was used for all three programs (NDSL, SEOG and CWS) and included the funds requested by the institution for each program for the forthcoming fiscal year. In accordance with regulations outlined by the U.S. Commissioner of Education as prescribed by the Higher Education Act of 1965 as amended, institutions were required to justify their request for funds by providing information on the total student enrollment, the number of students with financial need, the total cost of attendance, and the total resources available to students, and they were also required to supply narrative documentation of their ability to administer the funds requested.

Once the ten regional USOE offices had received the tripart applications from participating institutions, the applications were edited for mathematical and instructional correctness. Next, they were submitted to a regional panel for review. Regional review panels were usually composed of USOE personnel and professional student financial aid administrators sometimes augmented by an expert from a related area. The regional review panels normally took two working weeks to review all institutional requests for funds.

The review was performed in accordance with written criteria and instructions developed by the U.S. Office of Education. Each institution's tripart application was reviewed individually to determine whether the dollars that it had requested were reasonable when compared to the needs of similar institutions and also met general standards of reasonable educational costs and student resource expectations set forth in the panel instructions. The recommended funding levels for all three programs and an explanation of the reasons for any reductions in the amounts awarded from the funds requested were sent to the institutions. Institutions then either chose to accept the regional panel's recommendations or, if reductions had been made, they filed an appeal. The appeal process was initiated with the regional USOE officer, and, when necessary, further appeals could be directed to a national appeal panel.

Once the panel review process, including appeals, was completed, the total recommended funding levels for the nation, by state, were calculated, and Congress appropriated funds for each of the three programs. At this point, the state allotment formulas for each of the three programs became important. According to the appropriate section of the law for each program, the U.S. Commissioner of Education determined the state allotment for each state. It is important to note that application of the appropriate state allotment formula is a separate function in the total allocation process completely unrelated to the funding level recommended for the individual states and to the application and regional panel review process.

Once the actual state allotment of federal funds in the campus-based programs had been determined by use of the appropriate state allotment formulas, the next step was to determine the actual allocation of federal funds to each participating institution. First, the state percentage for each program was calculated as the actual state allocation divided by the state's total recommended funding level times 100. The resulting state percentage was then multiplied by the recommended funding level for each institution to determine the actual allocation of funds to the institutions participating in the programs. The sequence of events in the total allocation process is illustrated by the following flow chart, Figure 1.

In summary, four different state allotment formulas were involved in allocation of funds under the three programs. For the NDSL program, the allotment was based on postsecondary full-time enrollment; for initial SEOG, on postsecondary full-time equivalent; for continuing SEOG, on the ratio of total appropriations to total regional panel recommendations; and for CWS, on three equally weighed components: postsecondary full-time enrollment, high school graduates, and percentage of low-income family children. The base enrollment data used in determination of the state allotment percentages were obtained from the National Center for Education Statistics operated by the Education Division of the Department of Health, Education, and Welfare. Application of the ratio of the enrollment data set forth above, plus the 10 percent discretionary allowance, dictated the state's allocation, not the recommendations of the regional panel. The funding level recommended for each state by the regional panel was pertinent only to calculation of the state percentage for each program. The state percentage figure was necessary to calculate the actual total allocation of funds to individual institutions within a state. The funding level recommended by the regional panel for each institution within a given state was multiplied by the state's percentage figure to determine its allocation of funds for each appropriate program (McCormick, 1978).

To appreciate the effect of these formulas on the allocation of federal funds and to understand the new funding process for 1979–80 and 1980–81, three characteristics of the allocation process must be kept in

Figure 1. Institutional Allocation

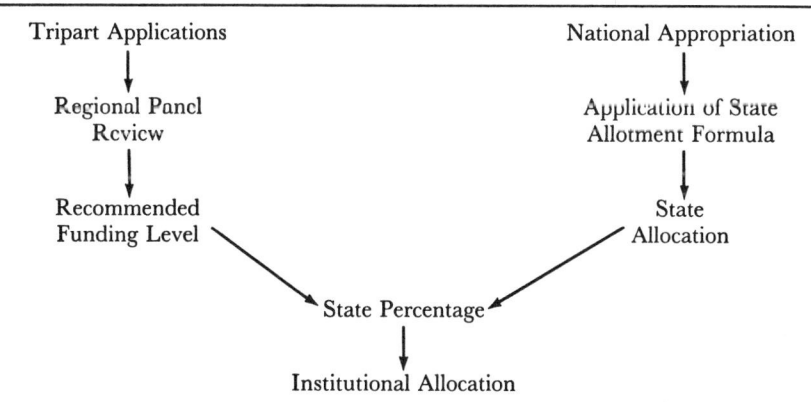

mind. First, the state allotment formulas are based on one major demographic variable, student population. Although there are different elements within each formula, each element represents a different categorical grouping of the same variable, student population. The single exception exists in the CWS allocation formula, which uses one socio-economic variable, the number of children from families with $3,000 or less in income.

Second, the state allotment formulas are statutory, set forth in the Higher Education Act of 1965, and thus they cannot easily be influenced or altered by the political process. The only way in which policymakers (Congress, the White House, USOE, interest groups, and so forth) can influence or affect the state allotment formulas is through the total national appropriations enacted for each program. Third, the actual allocation of total federal funds to a given state is in no way influenced or affected by the recommended funding level for that state.

The New Allocation Process

The panel of experts, primary architects of the new allocation process, developed the 1979-80 process with the following goals in mind (Huff, 1979):

- To phase in the new process over a period of years in order to prevent a sudden dislocation of funds from one state or institution to another.
- To streamline the process by the use of a formula and automated data processing to provide a more timely delivery of award letters to institutions.
- To utilize standard measurements of financial need derived from verifiable and auditable data for institutions.
- To develop a nationwide data base for institutions participating in the campus-based programs in order to analyze the results of the new funding process.
- To combine the fiscal operations report and the funding request in one document.
- To differentiate gift aid from self-help, which enables each institution to establish its need for gift aid independent of the level of self-help aid available to that institution.

The formula developed by the panel of experts for the distribution of campus-based funds to institutions was relayed to USOE with the strong recommendation that the formula approach be implemented over a minimum of three years in three phases: In Phase I (1979-80), the formula applies only to those institutions requesting funding above their conditional guarantee. In Phase II (1980-81), the conditional guarantee is reduced to 90 percent of the previous years' expenditures and all institutions are required to submit data to distribute more of the campus-based funds according to the formula. In Phase III (1981-82 or later), the conditional guarantee for all institutions would be abandoned and all funds would be allocated by formula.

Paramount to an understanding of the new formula process for the allocation of campus-based funds to institutions are its three major components: the state allotment formulas, the conditional guarantees, and the funding formulas used to determine each institution's fair share of the available funds. The three state allotment formulas, mandated by the Title IV legislation as amended, must be a part of this new allocation process. Thus, the conditional guarantees and the fair share formulas had to be developed within the framework of the statutory state allotment formulas.

Sections 174.3, 175.3, and 176.3 of the final regulations for NDSL, SEOG, and CWS (*Federal Register,* August 13, 1979) outline the requirements for the state allotment formulas. These formulas require that 90 percent of the national appropriation be distributed to the states, not to institutions, in proportion to the ratio of the state's student population to the national student population. In addition, each state must be funded at its individual "threshold" level of funding in each program. These threshold levels correspond to the states' actual appropriations for fiscal year 1972. Therefore, the first step in the allocation of campus-based funds to institutions is in no way related to the institution's application for funds or to the relative financial need of the institution. In other words, the state allotment formulas isolate the application and allocation process from the distribution of the great majority of funds to institutions within separate states. It is only the remaining 10 percent of the total national appropriation that institutions can apply for nationally.

As stated earlier, one of the goals of the new funding process was to prevent a massive redistribution of funds among institutions. Thus, each institution was first assigned a conditional guarantee of funds for each program. For the 1979-80 year, this conditional guarantee was calculated as the greater of two sums: The 1978-79 allocation multiplied by the 1977-78 utilization rate or the total funds expended in 1977-78.

Institutions then had the option of requesting only their conditional guarantee of funds or of submitting additional data and requesting additional funds above the conditional guarantee. Only those institutions requesting funding greater than the conditional guarantee and submitting additional data were considered for the additional funds available in each program.

The third major component of the new funding process was the formula used to determine an institution's fair share of the funds remaining after all conditional guarantees had been met. Remember, only institutions requesting funds greater than their conditional guarantees were involved in the distribution of these remaining funds. Prior to application of the formula, the institutions within an individual state were first considered for funding from the additional conditional guarantee funds if such funds existed for that state. The additional conditional guarantee funds would be available to institutions only within a state where the sum of all the conditional guarantees was insufficient to bring program funding to the level required by the statutory state allotment formula. The additional conditional guarantee funds available to a particular institution were assigned in the following manner:

$$\text{Total additional funds required to meet the state's allotment level of funding} \times \frac{\textit{Institution Index}}{\text{Total indexes in State}}$$

The *institutional index* is the relative need for funds in a particular campus-based program as calculated by the formula in the new funding process. It is calculated by use of the formula data submitted on the application for funds (enrollment, tuition, basic grant expenditures) and the application of those data to the formula for either the SEOG or the self-help programs (NDSL, CWS).

In reality, two formulas are used in the new process for allocation of campus-based funds. One formula relies on undergraduate data to calculate the SEOG index (the relative need of the institution for SEOG funds), and the other formula results in a self-help index (a measure of the institution's relative need for NDSL and CWS). The SEOG index is the difference between 70 percent of undergraduate aid applicants' cost and the sum of effective family contributions, basic grants, state scholarships, and 50 percent of the institutional scholarships and grants.

Since calculation of the SEOG index assumes that approximately 70 percent of undergraduate costs have been met by grants, scholarships, and effective family contributions, the undergraduate portion of the self-help is set as the lesser of two figures: 30 percent of undergraduate aid applicants' cost minus effective family contributions or undergraduate aid applicants' cost minus effective family contributions. The graduate student portion of the self-help index is the graduate aid applicants' cost minus effective family contributions. Therefore, the self-help index is the sum of undergraduate and graduate self-help indexes.

To understand the final step in the new funding process, the assignment of an institution's fair share funds, the following definitions should be noted: The institutional index is the relative financial need as derived by the formula for each program, the relative national index is the ratio of the institutional index in a particular program to the total indexes in that program for all schools, the institutional fair share is the product of the institution's relative national index and the total funds available for the particular program, the institutional shortfall is the amount by which an institution's fair share exceeds the funds already assigned to the institution, the institutional relative shortfall is the institution's shortfall divided by the total national shortfall, and the actual institutional fair share funds are the product of the institution's relative shortfall and unassigned funds.

From the above definitions it is clear that an institution's fair share funding depends primarily on the total funds available nationally after all conditional guarantees have been met and on the ratio of its index, its fair share, and its shortfall to the national total indexes, fair shares, and shortfalls. Thus, the total final allocation of funds to a given institution is the sum of the conditional guarantee, any additional conditional guarantee, and the actual fair share funds available to the institution (*Federal Register,* December 7, 1979).

The Campus-Based Allocation Process for 1980-81

The funding process for 1980-81 contains certain modifications, although the basic components were not altered. The modifications in the 1980-81 allocation formula are as follows (*Federal Register,* March 13, 1980).

Calculation of Conditional Guarantees. For the NDSL program, an institution's conditional guarantee is equal to the greater figure of two: 90 percent of actual 1978-79 expenditures or 90 percent of the product of NDSL expenditures for 1979-80 and the NDSL utilization rate for 1978-79. (It should be noted that there is no conditionally guaranteed federal capital contribution for NDSL; the federal contribution is a derived amount based on loan collections, cash on hand, and reimbursement income.)

For initial year SEOG program, the conditional guarantee is the greater of two figures: 90 percent of 1978-79 expenditures or 90 percent of the product of the 1979-80 allocation and the 1978-79 utilization rate. For the continuing year SEOG program, the conditional guarantee is calculated in the same manner, but the resulting guarantee figure is based on 100 percent. For the CWS program, the conditional guarantee is the greater of two figures: 90 percent of actual 1978-79 federal expenditures or 90 percent of the product of the 1979-80 federal allocation and the 1978-79 utilization rate. (The amounts calculated for SEOG initial and continuing guarantees represent the total SEOG conditional guarantee figure when combined. The actual conditional guarantee for initial year and continuing year funds is derived from the ratio of initial and continuing SEOG funds requested by the institution.) The basic formulas for calculating an institution's SEOG and self-help indexes remain the same. However, for 1980-81, all institutions are required to submit data needed for calculation of their fair share, while the application income grids have been expanded. For reporting formula data, the base year is 1978-79 in all categories, except for state scholarships and grants institutional scholarships and grants, which have a base year of 1977-78. The living expense allowance used in calculating the total educational cost is updated for 1980-81 to $2,600, from $2,450 for 1979-80. In 1980-81, an institution's loan repayment is to be 121 percent of the 1978-79 level, and funding for the federal capital contribution (FCC) to the NDSL fund will be met only if the institution has met one of the following conditions: its default rate is 10 percent or less, or its default rate was reduced by at least 25 percent from the preceding year, or the institution can clearly demonstrate the exercise of due diligence in the collection of loans. For 1980-81, the additional conditional guarantee funds for institutions is calculated from three factors: the institution's state fair share, which is defined as the amount mandated to the state by the product of the state allotment formula and the ratio of the institutional index to the total indexes of all institutions within the state; the institutional state shortfall, which is defined as the difference between the state fair share and the institution's conditional guarantee; and the relative state shortfall, which is defined as the ratio of the institutional state shortfall to the total shortfall within the state.

The actual additional conditional guarantee funds for an institution are calculated as the product of the relative state shortfall for that institution and the difference between the total state allotment and the total conditional guarantees for all institutions within the state. The practice of brokerage, whereby the funding for one self-help program is increased by requesting less funding for another self-help program, has been eliminated for 1980–81. Finally, according to the modifications for the 1980–81 academic year, no institution was to be awarded an allocation greater than that actually requested by the institution.

These modifications in the campus-based allocation process for 1980–81 were made primarily to move the allocation process closer to the new fair share concept of the distribution of funds. A complete explanation of the 1980–81 allocation formula process can be found in the March 13, 1980 issue of the *Federal Register*.

Funding Results and Final Comments

Owing to the complexities of the new formula process for the allocation of campus-based funds, the impact of statutory state allotment formulas, and the absence of reliable data, it is difficult to analyze the results of the new funding process. It is possible to examine the resulting allocations by state and by institutional type, but this does not tell us much. No attempt can be made in this chapter to analyze the data state by state. However, Table 1, which illustrates the distribution of funds by institutional type for the various programs, will allow the reader to examine the shift of funds from one sector to another.

As Table 1 shows, there does not appear to have been a major shift of campus-based funds from one sector to another in the first two academic years in which the new formula funding process was applied. There does appear to have been a gradual shift of funds in the College Work-Study program from the public sector to the private sector. However, the impact of this shift is somewhat offset by the $100 million increase in funding since 1978–79. In the SEOG and NDSL programs, there has been very little shift of funds between sectors.

An examination of total campus-based federal student aid allocations by state gives a somewhat different picture. By comparing total state allocations, one can easily see the movement of funds from one state to another. Based on a review of the tentative allocation of funds to states, there appears to be no major shifts of funds between states if the amount of increase or decrease is compared to the total national appropriation. Table 2 illustrates the distribution of funds for the various pro-

Table 1. Allocations to Campus-Based Federal Student Aid Programs by Institutional Type (in Thousands of Dollars)

	1978–79 Allocation	% of Total	1979–80 Allocation	% of Total	1980–81 Allocation	% of Total
NDSL: Federal Capital Contributions						
National Total	$310,353	(100.0)	$308,708	(100.0)	$280,075	(100.0)
Public Four-Year	$129,751	(41.8)	$127,886	(41.4)	$113,340	(40.5)
Public Two-Year	$ 11,806	(3.8)	$ 9,941	(3.2)	$ 15,135	(5.4)
Private Four-Year	$118,598	(38.2)	$125,475	(40.6)	$108,424	(38.7)
Private Two-Year	$ 4,187	(1.3)	$ 6,492	(2.1)	$ 6,006	(2.1)
Proprietary	$ 46,012	(14.8)	$ 38,914	(12.6)	$ 37,170	(13.3)
SEOG: Initial and Continuing Year Combined						
National Total	$269,960	(100.0)	$338,420	(100.0)	$362,415	(100.0)
Public Four-Year	$102,830	(38.1)	$126,678	(37.4)	$137,182	(37.9)
Public Two-Year	$ 37,468	(13.9)	$ 43,220	(12.8)	$ 51,424	(14.2)
Private Four-Year	$ 96,017	(35.6)	$127,763	(37.8)	$132,816	(36.6)
Private Two-Year	$ 7,569	(2.8)	$ 11,019	(3.3)	$ 11,419	(3.2)
Proprietary	$ 26,076	(9.7)	$ 29,740	(8.8)	$ 29,574	(8.2)
College Work–Study						
National Total	$433,800	(100.0)	$547,023	(100.0)	$537,749	(100.0)
Public Four-Year	$200,406	(46.2)	$235,730	(43.1)	$228,739	(42.5)
Public Two-Year	$ 82,418	(19.0)	$ 93,190	(17.0)	$ 89,461	(16.6)
Private Four-Year	$132,864	(30.6)	$194,344	(35.5)	$195,749	(36.4)
Private Two-Year	$ 10,454	(2.4)	$ 15,178	(2.8)	$ 14,506	(2.7)
Proprietary	$ 7,658	(1.8)	$ 8,580	(1.6)	$ 9,294	(1.7)

Source: Bureau of Student Financial Assistance, unpublished statistical report, March 1980.

grams by states in which allocations saw a sizable increase or decrease.

Although the total increase or decrease for the states in Table 2 is in excess of $1 million, the total dollars lost or gained do not represent more than 4 percent of the national appropriation in any program. Just what impact these shifts will have on institutions within these states is difficult to determine. The shifts result from the state allotment formulas, the conditional guarantees to individual institutions, and the total funds remaining for distribution on the basis of the new formula concept. The major data elements used in the new formula process to calculate an institution's relative financial need (gift aid and self-help indexes) also have an important effect on the final allocation of funds.

The resolve of the U.S. Office of Education to develop a new formula for the allocation of campus-based student aid funds is a noble effort, and the work of the panel of experts who developed the formula is

Table 2. Allocations to Campus-Based Federal Student Aid Programs by State

State	1979–80 Allocation	1980–81 Allocation	Change
NDSL: Federal Capital Contribution			
California	$31,862,843	$29,900,041	$ – 1,926,802
Kansas	$ 3,727,319	$ 2,516,764	$ – 1,210,555
Massachusetts	$16,004,478	$12,493,769	$ – 3,510,709
New York	$29,064,196	$26,028,717	$ – 3,035,479
Oregon	$ 6,106,926	$ 5,095,060	$ – 1,011,866
Pennsylvania	$15,314,292	$13,867,252	$ – 1,447,040
Texas	$10,452,401	$12,440,812	$ + 1,988,411
Washington	$ 7,394,836	$ 5,762,537	$ – 1,632,299
SEOG: Initial and Continuing Year Combined			
California	$33,497,680	$35,846,128	$ + 2,348,448
Massachusetts	$18,719,084	$19,610,360	$ + 891,276
New York	$25,473,635	$29,579,476	$ + 4,105,841
Pennsylvania	$18,604,672	$20,997,704	$ + 2,393,032
Texas	$15,353,758	$18,223,785	$ + 2,870,027
College Work-Study			
California	$48,897,918	$46,841,262	$ – 2,056,656
Massachusetts	$31,872,275	$29,072,317	$ – 2,799,958
New York	$47,994,301	$50,826,869	$ + 2,832,568
Oregon	$ 9,497,573	$ 8,409,655	$ – 1,087,918
Pennsylvania	$28,686,121	$27,114,989	$ – 1,571,132
Tennessee	$ 9,397,042	$10,530,297	$ + 1,133,255
Texas	$26,106,483	$28,113,801	$ + 2,007,318
Wisconsin	$12,876,751	$11,816,035	$ – 1,063,616

to be commended. This combined effort has already brought about notable improvements thanks to three factors: removal of much of the grantsmanship that existed under the old methodology, application of a more uniform standard for distribution of funds, and overall simplifcation of the process. Further refinements are needed to guarantee that the allocation process results in a reasonable and equitable distribution of funds to all institutions. Whether the needed refinements can be made is a subject of much debate and question. It is only to be hoped that the process will continue to improve.

References

Bureau of Student Financial Assistance. *Statistical Report.* Washington, D.C.: Bureau of Student Financial Assistance, March 1980.

Conrad, C., and Cosand, J. *The Implications of Federal Education Policy.* Washington, D.C.: ERIC Higher Education Research Reports, 1976.

Department of Education. *45CFR Parts 174, 175, 176, National Direct Student Loan, College Work-Study, and Supplemental Educational Opportunity Grant Program. Federal Register,* December 7, 1979, *44* (237), 70652-70662.

Department of Education. *45CFR Parts 174, 175, 176, National Direct Student Loan, College Work-Study and Supplemental Educational Opportunity Grant Program. Federal Register,* March 13, 1980, *45* (51), 16412-16436.

Huff, R. *The Final Report of the Panel of Experts.* Unpublished document, Washington, D.C., 1979.

McCormick, J. L. *State Allocations Formulas for Campus-Based Federal Student Aid Programs: A Descriptive Study.* Iowa City, Iowa: American College Testing Program, 1978.

Joe L. McCormick is executive director of the Texas Guaranteed Student Loan Corporation, formerly director of financial aid at the University of Houston, Central Campus; director of financial aid at Mississippi State University and past president of the National Association of Student Financial Aid Administrators.

Student aid research is not—or should not be—hard for the practitioner to do. Here are a few suggestions for why and how more aid administrators should add the term researcher *to the list of their functions.*

The Handyperson's Guide to Student Aid Research

William D. Van Dusen

Traditionally, participation in postsecondary education has been viewed as one of the major mechanisms for achieving equality of economic opportunity and for providing social mobility to minority groups of all kinds. Financial assistance to individual students, rather than to the institutions which students attend, has been the primary mechanism by which the federal government has helped to assure participation by those who are unable to do so by the state of their own resources. Since passage of the National Defense Education Act in 1959, the federal government has made available nearly $30 billion in direct aid to students through the basic, supplementary, and state grant programs; the College Work-Study employment program; and the national direct and guaranteed loan programs (U.S. Office of Education, undated). States, postsecondary institutions, and private donors also provide aid to students. For 1979–80, the total from all sources is estimated to be more than $14 billion (Van Dusen and O'Hearne, 1980). Estimates suggest that as many as 75 percent of the enrolled undergraduate students may qualify for some form of student aid.

Considering the level of expenditure and the number of individuals, families, and institutions affected by student aid programs, there has been very little coordinated effort to determine who receives assistance, who should receive assistance, how the assistance should be delivered, and what the long-range implications of student aid are or could be. The fall and winter 1978–79, issues of *College Student Personnel Abstracts* include eighteen entries under the general heading *financial aid,* but only half are data-based analyses. Of the more than 800 entries in a guide to the literature of student financial aid (Davis and Van Dusen, 1978) fewer than 200 appear under the heading *research on financial aid,* and many of these are the routine reports produced annually by the national need analysis services and by state scholarship and loan commissions.

Given that the modern history of student aid administration encompasses more than twenty years, the research identified in the aforementioned guide represents fewer than ten articles per year, or about one research article for every $150 million in student aid made available by the federal government. In some areas of investigation, the lack of research is particularly detrimental. Although total lending under the national direct and guaranteed loan programs exceeds $17 billion, the guide includes only one article describing the impact of borrowing on students' postgraduate activities.

Why Isn't More Done?

Many reasons can be postulated for the lack of research. One reason is the lack of training in research among student aid administrators. A recent survey (National Association of Student Financial Aid Administrators, 1978) reported that only 5 percent of responding aid directors had completed the doctoral level studies where research training typically takes place. Only 30 percent of those who responded to the survey said that their office had conducted any research in the preceding two years, and fewer than half of those said that their research study had employed a test of statistical significance.

Another reason for the lack of research is undoubtedly related to the absence of interest among postsecondary institutions themselves in providing support for research activities in and about their financial aid operations. Many senior administrators appear to believe that gift horses should not be looked in the mouth.

The professional educational research community also appears not to have been particularly active in the conduct of research on student aid. A few names, such as Astin, Bowman, Henry, and Nelson, appear with some frequency, but most of the work in the literature appears to be one-time efforts by individuals completing requirements for advanced degrees. Judging by the few directors of financial aid who have doctor's degrees, those who do conduct graduate-level research projects in financial aid either do not obtain degrees or quickly move on to some other endeavors.

Even if we grant that these reasons are valid, the fact remains that those in the best position to do student aid research—the student aid administrators of individual institutions—have not fully accepted the responsibility, which characterizes the members of other occupations recognized as professions, for the development and maintenance of a body of knowledge about their area of activity and expertise. It is toward changing that fact that this chapter is directed.

Where Does the Individual Start?

Research is part of the basic ongoing operational functions of federal and state governments. Their research agendas are largely set by public policy, and their research activities are funded by public appropriations and conducted, or at least directed, by public employees designated to that task. Private donors do not always have research as part of their programs, but if they do, it is typically funded. Even students conduct research as part of their academic programs. But the student aid administrator has more than enough to do simply to run the various programs for which he or she is responsible. How then does the student aid administrator become a researcher?

The hardest part of research is beginning it. Nevertheless, as Nelson's Ninth Law says, "the more you do it, the easier it gets" (Nelson, 1978). Producing research takes discipline. However, once that discipline is mastered, research activities can become a routine by-product of the normal day-to-day operations of a financial aid office. The names that appear again and again in the research literature are generally those of administrators who produced one article, found that it was not all that hard, began a second, then a third—and suddenly they were researchers.

Simply by virtue of their position of responsibility for the operations of institutional student aid programs, individual financial aid officers can identify the issues most in need of investigation. They can also identify issues which are—or which should be—since one of the most important outcomes of good research is to provide the answers to questions that no one knew needed to be asked—of interest to senior administrators at their institutions and to program administrators at the state and federal level. The most effective student aid administrators anticipate the important issues that will arise and work toward answers before being asked to do so.

The formal research training provided in graduate schools includes exposure to the elements of classical, formal research studies. These elements are appropriate and necessary in activities intended to present original contributions to the body of knowledge of a given academic discipline. But research intended for the world of action need not necessarily take such a rigorous course. One-page memoranda addressing single issues and offering specific and concrete steps for resolving them may be more appropriate than bulky documents that begin with extensive surveys of the literature. Action research does not require fancy statistics, which most audiences do not really understand and which often tend to discourage use of the reports in which they are included. Frequently, means, medians, and frequency distributions will illuminate what multivariate probit analysis may occult.

At the same time, student aid research studies need not be based on massive samples. Krejcie and Morgan (1970) assert that, to obtain results generalizable at a 95 percent level of confidence from a population of as many as 50,000, the sample requires only 381 individuals. That sample would, of course, have to be carefully constructed, and all those included in the sample would have to respond.

There are several basic questions that an aid administrator should ask when beginning a research project. Clear answers at the beginning can save time as the research proceeds, and they also help to guarantee that the product is worth the effort expended.

1. *What are the intended outcomes?* A study intended to change internal office policy can, and probably should, take a different approach and maintain a different level of rigor from a study intended to demonstrate to the dean of a college that he or she should allocate more money to grants for undergraduate students. A study intended to identify a problem in administration of the Basic Grant program and point to possible modifications of administrative procedure could be conducted differently from a study intended to demonstrate the long-term implications of large amounts of borrowing.

2. *Who is the intended audience?* Faculty in academic disciplines may react favorably to one kind of research, while administrative colleagues will prefer another kind of research. Ideally, research should appeal to as

wide a variety of audiences as possible in order to comply with another of Nelson's laws (1978), "Do it for more than one purpose." Data from a statistical report to the Office of Education can be excerpted for a memorandum to the president; sections of an article prepared for the *Journal of Student Financial Aid* can be reorganized for use in the alumni bulletin.

3. *What are the sources of data required to complete the study?* Historical data in the institution's files and archives are amenable to one kind of analysis and to solutions to some kinds of problems. Other problems and analyses require that original data be collected; frequently, such data will require complicated longitudinal research designs.

4. *What kinds of cooperation and support are required and available?* The research that is easiest to complete is that which can be done with the personnel resources of the individual administrator and the financial and informational resources of the aid office. It really is easier to do it yourself. Interinstitutional cooperation from peers may be easier to obtain than intrainstitutional cooperation from administrators unconcerned with the issue at hand. One hidden resource at many institutions is the pool of College Work-Study eligible graduate students who are looking for graduate thesis or dissertation topics. Part of the past disinterest shown by institutional research offices may be due simply to lack of requests for assistance.

5. *What analytical methods are appropriate and required?* Simple statistics may not be appropriate for certain kinds of research. To be successful and accurate, some projects may require statistical analyses beyond the capacity of the individual aid administrator. At many institutions, however, support may be forthcoming from the computer center, and sophisticated user-oriented statistical analysis packages may be readily available.

6. *Can the research be completed on time?* In some situations, partial information at the time it is needed may be more appropriate than complete information after the issue has been decided; other situations may demand full reporting and complete analysis if the research is to have any impact on decision making.

The answers to these questions, together with the research agenda developed by the aid administrator, can identify issues of importance which can be addressed with the resources available.

Two resources that can be harnessed in the conduct of student aid research deserve specific mention: the institution's computer information system and the administrator's colleagues at other institutions. Sanders (1979, p. 3) highlights the importance of communications with the administrators of computer systems: "To the extent that the [research] analyst can make wishes known when system changes are contemplated, or to the extent that proposed changes to the system are reviewed by the analyst, the operational system can be modified" to provide the information at the times and in forms that can facilitate research activities. Frequently, nothing more than a request is needed to assure that research data are maintained and retained.

Cooperative research involving peers at other institutions is another approach which can multiply the available interest and resources. Frequently, problems at one institution are significant at another. Generally, studies from two different institutions with similar results carry more weight in encouraging change than separate studies prepared in isolation. Some projects are particularly suited to a division of labor among several interested researchers. The resources of one institution, such as access to the computer for statistical analyses, may supplement those of another, such as graduate students available to collect large amounts of data. In many cases, the simple knowledge that another individual is working on a similar project may help the researcher to complete his or her own study.

The reason for undertaking research should not necessarily be to get a publication, but in the area of student financial aid, publication is generally easy to achieve. The *Journal of Student Financial Aid* has emerged as a respected document of record for the profession, yet its editors have difficulty filling its issues with sound research-based articles produced by practicing aid administrators (Huff, 1979). Other general purpose educational journals welcome submissions concerning financial aid. Even general circulation publications will accept articles about student aid. In many locales, the daily or weekly press is interested in information from and about the local college, and articles relating how students finance their educations at the college have particular appeal.

Publication need not be formal to be effective. A research study undertaken to tell the institution how it is doing or how it could be doing if it did things differently can be aired only within the institution and still be effective. It is likely, however, that what is or could be happening at one institution would interest colleagues at another institution. Sharing findings informally, but in writing, with colleagues at similar institutions or at institutions with similar problems can be a rewarding means of dissemination.

How To Get It Done?

Administration of student financial aid has been characterized as a partnership involving the federal and state governments, postsecondary institutions, private donors and agencies, and students. While student aid research has not always been considered in the development of that conceptual framework, it seems as though it should have been. Many of the research activities which need to be carried out cannot be managed efficiently, or at all, with the slow and cumbersome procedures involved in the issuance of federal requests for proposal, negotiation of fixed price contracts, Office of Management and Budget (OMB) clearance forms, and the other administrative trivia associated with federal research projects. Much research can and should be carried out by members of the partnership functioning at the state and local levels.

Implementation of the partnership in student aid research should begin with development of a preliminary agenda describing issues which need to be investigated. One association of student financial aid administrators attempted the development of such an agenda through a survey of its membership (Midwest Association of Student Financial Aid Administrators, 1978).

Each party to the student aid process would undoubtedly develop a somewhat different agenda, but it is likely that all the items on these individual agendas could be assigned to one of three major areas: who gets student aid and who does not, how aid eligibility and award amounts are determined, and outcomes realized as the result of student assistance at the postsecondary level. Each of these three areas can be studied from at least two focuses: policy research illuminates appropriate actions on a fundamental level, and program operation research demonstrates short-run implications. These two dimensions of research interest would combine to provide a structural framework as shown in Figure 1.

The question of changes in the way in which parental or student contributions to educational costs are determined could be considered by federal and state governments as a matter of public policy concerned with social equality and an adequately trained and educated populace. The same question could be considered by individual institutions as a matter of operations research to determine what institutional endowment income would have to be directed or redirected to student aid in order to maintain adequate levels of support for students. The question of how grant, loan, and work aid should be packaged could be consid-

Figure 1. A Conceptual Framework for Student Aid Research

Problem	Focus	
	Policy Research	Operations Research
Who gets aid? Who should?		
How is it distributed? How should it be distributed?		
What good does it do?		

ered as a problem of public policy to ensure the highest levels of persistence to program completion and as a matter of operational concern to determine how to minimize loss of tuition revenue as a result of premature attrition.

As with most other conceptual frameworks, the primary purpose of this framework is to place different research interests within a broad framework of investigation and to permit each potential researcher to see where his or her particular interests and competencies could best be directed. It could also serve to legitimize the publication of many internal studies, which could contribute to the body of knowledge about student aid but which have been suppressed by the administrators who conducted them because they did not consider the studies to be research. Questions which seem uninteresting from one focus may be fundamental to evaluation from the other focus.

Why Bother?

Arguments for the conduct of research by individual institutional aid administrators into their local populations and policies can be made from a base of the proper stewardship of funds or from a more general base of the social responsibility of educational institutions. They can also be made from the bottom line of enlightened self-interest.

The proper stewardship argument is perhaps the easiest to demonstrate and to understand. The individual institution possesses data unavailable from any other source. In the absence of the full-blown student information exchange suggested by the National Task Force on Student Aid Problems (1975), all reporting above the level of individual institutions will necessarily be summary in nature and eliminate much, if not most, of the information required for appropriate research activities. Further, the individual institutions already possess, or could if they wished to, information about one of the least studied and most important financial aid constituencies: students who do not apply for or who apply for and do not receive aid. One series of recent reports, for example, attempts to make the case that adult students, or their indistinguishable counterparts the part-time students, are grossly discriminated against in the award of aid. (See particularly, "Financing Part-Time Students: The New Majority in Post-Secondary Education." Washington, D.C.: American Council on Education, 1974, pp. 51-57.) Data available at the state and federal levels, however, make it impossible to substantiate or refute the charge. No information is available from state or federal sources on the age or course-load characteristics of the recipients of aid, and no information of any kind is available on the characteristics of nonrecipients of aid.

The social responsibility argument is characterized by what Lloyd-Jones and Smith (1954) describe in the title of their classical discussion of student personnel work as deeper teaching. Financial aid administrators who seek to be more than business office functionaries should concern themselves with the broader social and moral implications of their activities. As an editorial in the *Los Angeles Times* (1979) observed, "when one is talking about financial aid, one is in reality speaking of access to higher education — who'll get in and who won't, who'll go to the quality schools and who won't, who'll be equipped to lead in the future and who'll be consigned to follow." These statements seem to be well based, but the financial aid profession has yet to produce data to substantiate or refute them. At present, it is impossible to demonstrate that either the $14 billion in student aid available this year or the more than $30 billion that the federal government has provided since 1959 really have any influence on who becomes a leader.

It is the bottom line argument, however, that may be both the most compelling to individual administrators and the most successful in eliciting support from senior administrators. It is clear from the demographic data that the available pool of potential college students of traditional age will decline substantially during the next two decades, and colleges and universities will have to compete not only with each other but with civilian employers and the military for the reduced number of high school graduates projected for the 1980s (Henderson and Plummer, 1978). To the extent that financial aid will be a part of that competition, a better understanding of the dynamics which cause different students to apply, enroll, and persist will be required. This is particularly true of the dynamics and delivery of federal student aid, which now supplies 28 percent of the operating cost of postsecondary education (Education Department Bill Passed . . . ," 1979) and which can reasonably be expected to supply an even larger share in the future.

It will also be particularly important to know more about the real outcomes of participation in postsecondary education. Many believe that a college education has less economic value now than it did in the past (Freeman, 1976). Potential students may begin to demand demonstration of positive outcomes before they are willing to accept the substantial burden of nongrant assistance and to forgo earnings during the years required for completion of a degree program.

By way of conclusion, it may be said that a better understanding of the dynamics of the student aid process and a demonstration of its positive outcomes could well become a survival need for American postsecondary institutions in the next two decades. While it might be philosophically more pleasing to have student aid research conducted for purely generous reasons, necessity will require individual student aid administrators to demonstrate and document with hard facts and research data both the worth of and need for what they do. Every administrator will have to assume a larger share of responsibility for development and maintenance of the profession's body of knowledge if the profession and the administrator are to survive.

References

Davis, J. S., and Van Dusen, W. D. *Guide to the Literature of Student Financial Aid.* New York: College Entrance Examination Board, 1978.

"Education Department Bill Passed by Senate, Advanced in the House." *Higher Education and National Affairs,* 1979, *28* (18), 3.

Freeman, R. B. *The Declining Economic Value of Higher Education and the American Social Systems.* New York: Aspen Institute for Humanistic Studies, 1976.

Henderson, C., and Plummer, J.C. "Adapting to Changes in the Characteristics of College Age Youth." *American Council on Education Policy Analysis Series Reports,* 1978, *4* (2).

Huff, R. *The Final Report of the Panel of Experts.* Unpublished document, Washington, D.C., 1979.

Krejcie, R. W., and Morgan, D. W. "Determine Sample Size for Research Activities." *Educational and Psychological Measurement,* 1970, *30,* 607–610.

Lloyd-Jones, E. M., and Smith, M. R. *Student Personnel Work as Deeper Teaching.* New York: Harper & Row, 1954.

Los Angeles Times, February 27, 1979.

Midwest Association of Student Financial Aid Administrators. *Research Committee Membership Survey,* 1978.

National Association of Student Financial Aid Administrators. *Characteristics and Attitudes of Financial Aid Administrators.* Washington, D.C.: National Association of Student Financial Aid Administrators, 1978.

National Task Force on Student Aid Problems. *Final Report.* Brookdale, Calif.: National Task Force on Student Aid Problems, 1975.

Nelson, J. A. "Research That I Can or Should Do." Paper presented at annual meeting of the College Entrance Examination Board, New York, October 1978.

Sanders, L. E. "Dealing with Information Systems: The Institutional Researcher's Problems and Prospects." *The AIR Professional File,* Summer 1979, No. 2.

Van Dusen, W. D., and O'Hearne, J. J. *Design for a Model College Aid Office.* (3rd ed.) New York: College Entrance Examination Board, 1980.

William D. Van Dusen does contract research for postsecondary educational institutions, associations, and agencies.

The choice of a college or university and a course of study is a significant decision for the prospective student. In a move to ensure the availability of adequate information on which to base that decision the federal government has mandated that certain information be provided to all prospective students by institutions that receive federal Title IV financial assistance funds.

Student Consumer Information: The Right to Know— The Responsibility to Learn

Samuel Howell

Rarely have postsecondary institutions had such an opportunity as that now provided by the federal government. Postsecondary institutions are required to supply minimal information regarding financial aid, academic programs, and institutional data, but the costs of supplying this information may be met from the administrative expense account of campus-based financial aid programs. (The administrative expense is a 4 percent allowance paid by the federal government to institutions for the purpose of deferring the cost of administration of the campus-based programs.) That is to say, institutions are now funded to provide consumer information to prospective and enrolled students.

However, it has been difficult to design information systems that can be updated on a frequent basis. This difficulty is increased by the complexity and ever-changing status of most financial aid programs. To review the growth of student consumer information provides a basis on which to review the sources of data that are available to the financial aid administrator.

Are Students Consumers?

There appear to be differences of opinion on whether students may indeed be labeled consumers. Regardless of the nomenclature, however, the student does have a right to accessible financial aid information. If students and parents are expected to make decisions regarding postsecondary education, ample information must be provided to them for comparison and analysis.

There has been much discussion of the relationship between student consumerism and higher education. Young (1978) related consumerism to delivery of the product to the student and recommends that disclaimers be added to the rules and regulations in catalogues stating that policies at institutions do change. El-Khawas (1977) states that, unlike other consumer goods, a specific product cannot be expected for the student consumer. Many educators are concerned (USOE, 1978; Stark and others 1977, p. 67) with using the term "student as a consumer" since the student is an active participant in the education process. Others (John, 1977) point out that the basic purposes of student consumerism are protection from abuses, better selection by students, and assurance of program quality. Knight and Schotten (1977) also question promoting the student consumerism movement as it relates to higher education.

In regard to the kinds of information the students need, Hoy (1977) suggests three: access information, process information, and results information for future graduates. He also emphasizes that institutional personnel should not attempt to use statistics or facts to confuse students. This suggests that institutions should concentrate their efforts on providing financial aid information in a form which will permit students to compare the costs of education at various institutions. If understandable information was available, students and parents could make an informed decision on the options available to them. Potential students also require clear and ample information on the process involved in applying for financial aid. Finally, information pertaining to the futures that await the graduates of particular educational fields would round out student needs for institutional information.

The role played by the federal government in recent years shows that it is an ally of the student (Vaughn, 1977, p. 8). In fact, it is likely that the consumer movement will stay around for a while as it becomes focused on the objective of more and better information (Halstead, 1979, p. 30). The consumer movement has transformed a seller's market into a buyer's market, and students are beginning to think of themselves as consumers (Chapman, 1978, p. 25). It should be noted, however, that some institutions view the federal government's role as intrusive (Stark and others, 1977, p. 59). These institutions feel that certain of their responsibilities are student-centered, because the student is an active participant in the educational process. The federal government regulations place the liability for the dissemination of information on the institution. Nonetheless, students should have access to ample financial aid information for their decision-making process.

Financial Aid and the Student

In no other sector of higher education has the importance of student consumer information been stressed as it has in the sector of student aid. Institutions participating in Title IV programs that receive administrative allowances must assign first priority to the expenditure of funds to meet the requirements for student consumer information and dissemination ("Use of Funds," 1979, pp. 47466, 47489, 47504). Since the president of an institution normally signs the terms of agreement to participate in Title IV programs, the president has the ultimate responsibility, shared with the governing board, to assure compliance with this regulation. Within the individual university's organizational structure, however, it is typically the director of financial aid who has the specific responsibility to fulfill this requirement. What type of information should the director make available to students?

The need for improved communication between students and institutions regarding student financial aid is apparent. The Southern Association of Student Financial Aid Administrators (1978) stressed the need for accurate and meaningful information that would enable students and parents to make decisions. This group also indicated that a well-informed citizenry can help institutions to reach their goals and objectives.

Quality of Information. According to Chapman (1978), the quality of the information made available to student consumers should be improved. In a summary report on accreditation and the protection of the student consumer (USOE, 1978), it is stated that there is a "lack of necessary disclosure in writing" regarding not only financial aid but also other institutional policies such as refunds. Students stressed (CSS, 1976, p. 26) that lack of information was a common problem and that they needed "good" information. They further stated there was no way to plan ahead and that there had been a general lack of coordination among student services regarding information about the institutions and about institutional services. The same students also indicated a need for better counseling about their rights and responsibilities. According to Stark and others (1977, p. 8), "students who suffer most from . . . fraud . . . are least sophisticated in making judgments . . . ." The same authors indicate that consumer information should enhance educational choice and improve decision making. Again, there is a need for useful, concise information presented in a manner to enable potential students to compare several institutions.

FIPSE. In response to the need for better information, the National Task Force for Better Information for Student Choice was funded in 1975 by the Fund for the Improvement of Postsecondary Education (FIPSE) (Chapman, 1978, p. 25). This task force consisted of eleven institutions and four resource agencies. During the period of 1975–1977, the project sought to identify needs for better student information. As a result of its study, a variety of models for information was developed. In 1977, FIPSE funded a three-year project called the Center for Helping Organizations Improve in Education (Project CHOICE). The purpose of Project CHOICE was to proceed with the development of information models and to provide a clearinghouse for educational consumer information. The project had three areas of emphasis: to provide an audiovisual, newsletter, technical manual, and advice service; to work with nineteen colleges in revising their literature and to study the impact of the revised literature; and to provide a national linking service. Project CHOICE has provided excellent service in the development of better educational information to students, and those institutions which participated in Project CHOICE continue to serve as models of financial aid information.

Adequate Information. In a report on providing better financial aid information to students, it is (CSS, 1976, p. 19) concluded that students who need financial aid to meet educational costs frequently do not receive the information necessary to make a choice and that the complexity of the financial aid process was a primary problem for students with inaccurate or insufficient information. A large number of students indicated that they wanted it early in their school education. Of course, the problem is further compounded by the ever-changing programs and program regulations, which place a further burden on the financial aid administrator to implement a financial aid information system in which periodic revision and updating is possible.

The Federal Government and Student Information

The regulations regarding student consumer financial aid information were published in December 1977. As the *Federal Register* ("Information Dissemination . . .", 1977, p. 61406) summarizes these regulations, "Each institution which receives an administrative cost allowance for an award period shall . . . prepare material . . . and disseminate that information . . . to enrolled or prospective students who request all or part of that material." The regulations further require institutions to provide detailed information in several specific areas, including descriptions of all student financial aid programs, including Title IV, state, and institutional programs; the procedures and forms used in making applications for the various programs; a statement of student rights and responsibilities, which includes the continuing eligibility requirements, the criteria for good standing and reestablishment of good standing, the method and frequency of payments to students, the terms of loans and a sample repayment schedule, and the terms and conditions of employment awarded as financial aid; the cost of attending for students living at home, on campus and off campus, including tuition and fees, books and supplies, room and board, and transportation; the refund policy; a description of the academic program, including current degree programs, other educational training programs, institutional laboratory and physical facilities, and faculty or other institutional personnel; data on the student retention rate; data on the number and percentage of students completing programs, if available; and the titles of persons who will disseminate the information.

Paragraph 178.6 of the December 13, 1979 issue of the *Federal Register* ("Use of Funds," 1979) indicates that the first use of the administrative cost allowance must be to meet the consumer information requirements and that only the remaining portion may be used for administration of the programs. The consumer costs must be documented, since these auditable data are reviewed when a compliance audit is conducted for the programs, and institutions must repay the funds if they cannot prove that funds were expended to fulfill student consumer information requirements. Minimum information must be provided to students.

Financial Aid Information Documents. Once the information has been gathered, it must be presented to students in a meaningful way. Institutions are not required by regulations to provide financial aid inforation in a single document. However, one phase of a comprehensive financial aid information system should include one document which contains a comprehensive review of financial aid. Information must be provided not only to prospective students but also to enrolled students who request it. All students who receive financial aid should have access to minimal information and any additional information pertinent to attendance at the institution. For these reasons, institutions should consider providing the required financial aid information, except for the data on academic programs and additional information on money management and related topics in a single document. The versatility of such a document is conducive to meeting the information needs of a variety of groups, including students and parents. The primary advantage of using a single document to meet the requirements is that all required information may be made available to the student from a single source.

Useful Information. The purpose of any student consumer information document should be to provide useful information to students (Southern Association of Student Financial Aid Administrators, 1978). This document should be in a form which will allow students to compare the information which it contains with information from other institutions. Further, the information must be factual, complete, and accurate. Costs of attendance should be based on documented research by the financial aid office. Institutional personnel should exercise caution in providing an awesome array of statistical data that might result in misinterpretation or a complete lack of understanding by the student. Therefore, when statistical data are provided, a clear and concise interpretation of the data should also be included.

Designing a Financial Aid Information System

Meeting the minimum requirements as outlined in the regulations should be only one of a series of activities aimed at providing better financial aid information to students. The task then becomes one of designing a complete financial aid information system.

Stark and others (1977) identify three stages in the process of building a prospectus: the research stage, the production stage, and the feedback stage. The institution's financial aid director must first identify the vehicle which will design a consumer information system. This vehicle may be the student aid staff, a student financial aid committee, a student affairs committee, the director of student aid, a student group, or a combination of these sources. Whatever mechanism is used, student input is a necessity and should be given primary consideration. The student perspective on financial aid can best be obtained if students are involved in the process from the initial stages (Halstead, 1979, p. 8).

Initial Review and Research. The first consideration of the individuals and groups designing the system will be to review the institution's goals and philosophy. The goals of the student financial aid office should also be reviewed, and they should coincide with and complement the goals of the institution. These goals should provide clarity and assist in identifying the population that the institution serves. The population served may vary from a specific group, as is the case on a residential campus, to the total community.

In addition, a preliminary calendar should be established to enable the document production procedure to be structured and scheduled and the procedure must begin early enough that the document may be completed in time to prove its usefulness. The actual or potential student population must be identified. Such factors as age, classification level (that is, undergraduate, graduate, and so forth), level of comprehension, and other student characteristics must also be identified to enable the institution to respond to the needs of its various subpopulations and to design a system that will receive maximum utilization by students.

Current and past institutional publications and information-sharing techniques should be reviewed. These publications and techniques may include, but are not limited to, financial aid brochures, audiovisual programs, and related institutional materials. At the same time, an evaluation should be conducted to determine the techniques that are most effective in providing information. This evaluation of current techniques will serve as a base for building the new information system.

Stark and others (1977) stress the importance of determining what students, educators, parents, and other publics believe that students should know. For example, parents feel that information on the financial resources needed for a student to obtain an education at a given institution is essential.

Institutional Resources. After a thorough review and evaluation of the current information, a decision can be made on the available options or methods of supplying information to students; that is, on design of a complete student information system. Several institutional resources may be used in developing material for student information use.

Student Groups. Student leaders, student organizations, and student honor groups can be beneficial in identifying student informational needs, and they can also assist in evaluating proposed student designs for student information. Before any document is printed, field testing should be conducted using students as evaluators. Student review may indicate areas that need clarification or areas in which additional information is required. Student review is critical to the development of any publication.

Financial Aid Committee. As mentioned previously, an experienced and operational financial aid committee may serve not only as an advisory group but also as the coordinating body for a student financial aid information system, collecting data on such things as students' expenses or assisting in the development and writing of actual publications.

Student Aid Staff. There is no better source of information on student needs than the student aid staff. This includes not only professional staff but support staff and student peer counselors. Indeed, student peer counselors whose primary responsibility is information dissemination may be one of the most effective means of transmitting information to students (Olson and Stegura, 1977-78, p. 19). However, for student peer counselors to be effective, they should receive adequate preparation, have limited responsibilities, and be accountable to a professional staff member. Students who have an understanding of financial aid programs and applications may serve as excellent facilitators of the financial aid processes and procedures.

Multimedia Center. Multimedia staff can provide direction in the production of various information programs on financial aid.

Art Department. The institution's art department may contribute designs, photographs, and drawings that will contribute to an effective and attractive information document or program. Consideration should be given to the use of College Work-Study students who are majoring in drawing, art, and so forth in design and production of the various student aid publications.

Business Office. Business office personnel can provide current information on tuition and fee structure, residential room and board costs, and other fee schedules in effect at the institution. Also, refund information, payment dates, and disbursement procedures are typically processed through the business office, and this information must be made available to students to meet the consumer information requirements.

Admissions/Registrar. The staff of the admissions/registrar's office may provide input on admission procedures, academic criteria, and time schedules of the institutional calendar.

Placement Center. Placement center personnel serve as the primary source of information and data on graduates and the placement and employment record of students.

Draft Outline. After a thorough search of information has been conducted, an outline of the student information system should be drafted for review by the several populations mentioned previously. It is likely that the reviewers will propose changes.

The initial review of the information system should be made by the student aid staff and the committee or groups that initiated and produced the various documents and systems. Input and evaluation should be sought from as many sources as possible.

One portion of the student information system must be an informational brochure or booklet. At this point in the production process, a decision must be made regarding the design and format of that document, and such variables as size, color, cost, and form must be determined. Consideration may be given to a newspaper format, which has the obvious advantages of low cost and frequent updating to maintain the currency of the information presented.

Utilization of the document must be taken into consideration when both the content and design are decided. Is the document to serve the needs of prospective students, enrolled students, or nontraditional students? The document should be readable, to encourage student use. As mentioned previously, the document should be field-tested to determine its effectiveness prior to final production. Draft copies may be provided to student groups, selected parents, prospective high school students, and institutional personnel for critical review.

No institution should rely on only one method for a student consumer information system; alternate sources of information should always be considered. Other possible methods of disseminating information include slides, slide-tapes, and closed circuit television and audiovisual tape.

The use of slides enables the aid administrator to vary the presentation to suit student needs. This method also allows information to be updated. Slides are relatively inexpensive compared to other media and they are versatile in that they may be used in an automated presentation to individuals or large groups.

Institutional aid personnel may have access to slide-tape units on which information may be preprogramed for use. This type of presentation is particularly effective for preloan counseling and exit interviews relevant to institutional loan programs and aid application processes.

Institutions equipped with closed circuit television equipment may produce effective programs to meet various student needs. Lack of available production equipment and staff may limit broad use of this medium, but institutions with adequate facilities and staff can utilize this as an excellent source of information dissemination. Lack of closed circuit television and audiovisual tape devices will also limit the use of this method.

A plan should be implemented to guarantee continuous updating and evaluation of the student information system that is established. If students deem the system nonproductive, it is appropriate to alter the system or to design a new information system. Changes in regulations and procedures require, at a minimum, an annual review of the student information system. It has been recommended (DHEW, 1979, p. 7) that audits be conducted to measure the qualities of various information designs. Whether the evaluation consists of audit, evaluation, or review, some type of evaluation system should be designed to measure the effectiveness of any information.

Development of an effective information system requires planning and maximum utilization of resources, but institutional aid administrators must view this challenge as an effective means of assisting students in the decision-making processes of higher education.

Summary

Acknowledgement is made of the fact that it is difficult to suggest a single system for providing financial aid information to students. Institutions differ greatly in size, type, and location and prospective and enrolled students are equally diverse. The situation is one that provides interesting challenges to individuals vested with the responsibility of providing financial aid information. Although there is not total agreement on the definition of the student as a consumer, financial aid administrators are still required to provide minimal information to the student.

Institutional personnel should develop a variety of financial aid information sources. The best of these sources are developed on the institutional campus. Once a system of informational sources has been developed, an evaluation should be performed to measure the effectiveness of the information. Students' utilization of these data will enhance their decisions regarding higher education.

(*Editor's Note:* Legislation currently under consideration by the House Senate Conference Committee may eliminate the requirement to spend administrative allowance first for student consumer purposes. However, there will continue to be an emphasis placed on clear and complete information concerning financial aid for students and their parents.)

References

Chapman, D. "Improving Information for Student Choice: The National Effort." *National Association of College Admission Counselors Journal,* 1978, *23* (1), 25-26.

College Scholarship Service (CSS). *Making It Count: A Report on Providing Better Financial Aid Information to Students.* New York: College Entrance Examination Board, 1976.

College Scholarship Service, Student Advisory Committee. "What 250 Student Say About Financial Aid Problems." *College Board Review,* 1976, (100), pp. 14-25.

El-Khawas, E. H. "Putting Student Consumer Issue in Perspective." *Educational Record.* 1977, *58* (2), 169-179.

Halstead, C. P. "Better Information for the Prospective Students." *College Board Review,* 1979, (112), pp. 8, 30.

Hoy, J. C. "Consumer Interests in Higher Education." *Educational Record,* 1977, *58* (2), 180-190.

"Information Dissemination Requirements." *Federal Register,* December 1, 1977, p. 61406.

John, L. G. "Student Consumer Protection in Postsecondary Education." *NASPA Journal,* 1977, *15* (1), 39-49.

Knight, G. A., and Schotten, P. "Effect of Consumer Movement on Universities." *North Central Association Quarterly,* 1977, *51* (4), 377-384.

Olson, L., and Stegura, D. "Students Counsel Students in Financial Aid Offices." *College Board Review,* 1977-78, (106).

Southern Association of Student Financial Aid Administrators. *Student Consumer Information.* 1978.

Stark, J. S., and others. *The Many Faces of Educational Consumerism.* Lexington, Mass.: Lexington Books, 1977.

U.S. Department of Health, Education, and Welfare (DHEW). "Students Helping Students." *Final Report of the Second Student/Commissioner Conference on Federal Financial Aid.* Washington, D.C.: DHEW, February 1979.

U.S. Office of Education (USOE). *Summary Report on Accreditation and the Protection of the Student as Consumer.* Washington, D.C.: Division of Eligibility and Agency Evaluation, U.S. Office of Education, 1978.

"Use of Funds." *Federal Register,* August 13, 1979, pp. 47466, 47489, 47504.

Vaughn, G. B. "Consumerism and the Community College." *Community and Junior College Journal,* 1977, *47* (6), 8-10.

Young, D. P. "The Registrar, the Admissions Office, and Academic Consumerism." *College and University,* 1978, *106,* 153-163.

Samuel Howell is director of financial aid at the University of Arkansas at Little Rock.

If professional financial aid counselors are not helping aid recipients to get off scholastic probation, perhaps they should step aside and let peer counselors show them how it can be done.

Peer Counseling: Can It Save Financial Aid Recipients on Scholastic Probation?

Jesús Gómez
Roberto Treviño-Martínez

During the decade of the 1970s, many colleges and universities throughout the country experienced symptons of cardiac arrest. We refer to the heart-rending pressure as they tried to address the needs of economically and educationally disadvantaged students while at the same time maintaining traditionally high academic standards. The sources of such pressure include charges by needy students and their advocates that equal educational opportunity is a myth and that colleges are not sensitive to the multifarious needs of the disadvantaged population, complaints from teaching faculty and administrators that disadvantaged students lack the basic skills for academic success in colleges, and warnings from trustees and alumni against the lowering of academic standards. Institutions must face this pressure against a backdrop of declining enrollments, alarming budget cuts, and reductions in state and federal funding.

This chapter focuses on a common dilemma of many financial aid administrators, that is, watching helplessly as needy recipients of financial assistance drop out of school after two semesters because of poor grades. This situation results, in part, from the relationship between extreme financial need and educational disadvantage, and it is complicated by federal regulations which require that recipients of federal aid be in good academic standing and make satisfactory progress in their course of study (U.S. Department of Health, Education, and Welfare, 1979). The Catch 22 is that these students are not eligible for financial assistance unless they are making satisfactory progress and cannot receive the academic help they need to show progress unless they receive the financial assistance that will allow them to finance continued enrollment.

In this chapter, student-to-student counseling is described in substantial detail as a highly effective intervention technique for assisting recipients of financial aid who are on scholastic probation and as a prevention technique for helping students receiving financial aid for the first time. There are at least two good reasons for using peer counselors in student financial aid offices. First, student financial aid offices, like other student services offices, are seldom staffed at a level equal to the work load. Although compensation is recommended for peer counselors, they are generally paid less than professional student aid counselors. In addition, many qualify for the College Work-Study program and thus can receive 80 percent of their wages from CWS program funds. Second, students respond positively to advice and counsel from peer counselors if those counselors are well trained and helpful.

Looking Back at Financial Aid

Between passage of the Higher Education Act of 1965 and the Education Amendments of 1976, the emphasis was placed on providing access to needy students rather than on institutional responsibility for administration of programs. Regulations were minimal, and the Office of Education responded to questions regarding program eligibility by referring the aid administrator to the statutes.

This period of minimum federal control ended with the Higher Education Amendments of 1976. As the size and complexity of aid programs increased and as evidence of waste, fraud, and abuse in the programs accumulated, participating institutions saw a marked decrease in their administrative freedom and autonomy (Van Dusen, 1979). Today, accountability is not only expected but required of institutions. In fact, government direction has expanded to such a degree that in many circles it is now viewed as overregulation. Requirements of student consumerism, academic good standing, and reasonable progress are lucid, present-day examples of federally mandated standards for administration of financial assistance programs by participating institutions.

Effects on Institutional Aid Offices

Increased government regulations continue to affect the operations of individual aid offices dramatically as traditionally understaffed offices are given additional responsibilities. Many changes in federal regulations require additional staff and changes in processing systems that most financial aid offices are ill-equipped to handle, at least in the short time for change allowed by the regulations.

A concomitant problem for aid offices has been the steady increase in financial aid applicants. Two factors have contributed to this increase: improvements in information dissemination to the eligible population, and the increased cost of a college education coupled with dwindling purchasing power as the result of inflation.

The increase in student applicants created by the factors just mentioned has been somewhat gradual but there are also events that bring about almost immediate crises. The Middle Income Student Assistance Act (MISAA) of 1978, for example, had an unprecedented impact on the financial aid community as middle-income students became eligible for financial assistance. The Office of Education served shocking notice to participating institutions: "Preparations should be already underway to handle the additional applications, questions, aid packages, and appeals that MISAA will bring. For some institutions, the number of applicants will double population on some form of student aid" (U.S. Department of Health, Education, and Welfare, 1979, p. 4). MISAA did indeed have a significant, if not shattering, impact on all phases of institutional operations—human resources, physical facilities, and time.

The experience of 1978 illustrates very clearly how extant systems of operation can be tested to their physical and temporal limits and how overloads and backlogs often result. The most damaging effect, however, is felt in the most important of all areas, that is, human resources. A systemic reality of institutions, and especially of the larger ones, is their wait-and-see approach to additional funding to head off such crises as the one created by MISAA in 1978. Since resources are limited, many institutions can ill afford to commit funds on forecasts. The net result is that financial aid offices find themselves operating under crisis conditions at times when they can least afford to. When additional demands are placed on offices that are already understaffed and overworked, morale and stress spiral in opposite directions. Low morale is manifested in high staff turnover, absenteeism, poor quality of work, and backlogs of financial aid applications. Staff turnover is especially critical because of the paucity of experienced, well-trained replacements in this relatively new and increasingly technical field and because of the time and energy that experienced staff must direct to the training of new staff at a time when their experience and expertise are required by the crisis. The result, of course, is a reduction in the quality and quantity of student services that are provided. It is not uncommon to see more and more professional staff shifting their service focus away from student contacts and toward paperwork. The resultant deterioration of student services seems particularly ironic in light of the fact that it was precipitated, in part, by legislation calling for more and better services for the student consumer.

Financial Aid: What It Is Supposed to Be

Certainly, the purpose of a financial aid office is not merely to process forms and disburse money to students, it should also be congruent with the philosophy and goals of higher education. Johnson and Frambs (1979) assert that the primary function of the financial aid counselor is to assist students with financial problems to enable them to pursue their educational goals. However, it is extremely important to remember that financial aid matters extend beyond the strictly fiscal. As these same authors point out, financial aid counselors should involve students in deeply personal ways, teaching them to ask questions of value, and purpose. This implies that an institution's financial responsibility to a student is also one of a personal nature. This interpretation is supported by Pernal (1977), who found that students strongly resent college officials who devote little time to them and truly respect and appreciate officials who take time to develop relationships with students and help them with individual problems and concerns. Obviously, a task for financial aid administrators is to find effective ways of meeting the burgeoning administrative demands of aid programs while at the same time providing better services to students. One workable vehicle all too often overlooked is paraprofessional assistance and, more specifically, the use of students as paraprofessional counselors.

Student-to-Student Counseling in Financial Aid

Although the concept of student-to-student counseling dates back to the mid-1960s (Brown, 1974), the idea of using student counselors was not seriously considered by financial aid administrators until the passage of the Education Amendments, Public Law 94-482, in 1976. The "Student Aid Information Service" section of this legislation made the Commissioner of Education responsible for ensuring that institutions employ "part-time financial aid counselors under work-study programs" and that "whenever possible [they] include student peer counselors . . . in training programs sponsored by the Office of Education" (Sec. 493B, 90 Stat. 2149). Since that time, studies have projected that well over 10,000 students and part-time workers are employed in more than 2,800 college aid offices throughout the United States (National Student Educational Fund (NSEF), 1976 and National Center for Education Statistics, 1977, cited in Stegura and Olson, 1977-78, pp. 19-20. The same investigations show that, of the 8,400 students involved, a projected 80 percent are employed through the College Work-Study program.

However, the manner in which students are being utilized by aid offices falls far short of the spirit of Public Law 94-482. In fact, the 1976 NSEF survey points out that more than 80 percent of the students working in aid offices at the time of the study were performing clerical duties and that only 27 percent had counseling or supervisory functions of any kind (Stegura and Olson, 1977-78, p. 20). These are disappointing in view of the Office of Education's finding that between 91 and 98 percent of the financial aid administrators polled in its 1977 survey were pleased with the job performance of their part-time student counselors (Stegura and Olson, 1977-78, p. 19). The obvious concern, of course, is that the student employee is viewed as little more than inexpensive clerical help; clearly, to use students only in this capacity is to shortchange both the aid office and the student. Thus, while critics of student-to-student counseling may argue that the financial aid field has become too technical or complain about high student employee turnover, available research does not support this skepticism. In fact, one of the most significant findings of the 1976 NSEF survey was that almost 50 percent of the students working in aid offices were in their "second (or more) year" of financial aid office experience (Stegura and Olson, 1977-78, p. 20).

While peer counseling is a relatively new phenomenon in the area of financial aid, much use has been made of students as paraprofessional counselors in other areas, such as academic and personal crisis counseling. One model for paraprofessional counseling is described in the *Training Manual for Paraprofessional and Allied Professional Programs* (Delworth and Aulepp, 1976). The effectiveness of paraprofessional counselors in academic advising has been documented by many, including Brown and others (1971). Much of Brown's (1974) research in the last fifteen years indicates that trained student paraprofessionals are indeed as effective as professional counselors in facilitating positive changes in student counselees and that counseling by student paraprofessionals can be effective, acceptable, practical, and adaptable.

The issue then becomes one not of whether financial aid offices can adapt the concept of student-to-student counseling to improve their services to students but whether they will do so. While there is much support for peer counseling in financial aid (College Scholarship Service, 1976; Public Law 94-482; Stegura and Olson, 1977-78; and Peterson and others, 1978), little empirical data exist to encourage aid offices to commit time, money, and human resources to the venture. In fact, there is hardly any literature that focuses specifically on peer counseling programs in offices of student financial aid. The handful of articles on the subject may be placed in one of three categories: needs assessments based on statistical surveys, suggested uses for peer counselors in financial aid offices, and suggested frameworks for setting up peer counseling programs.

Because the need for peer counselors in aid offices is no longer moot, the attention of administrators now turns to the two last concerns. The CSS Student Advisory Committee (1976) and the National Center for Education Statistics (1977) note that students are already being used in such areas as information dissemination, preliminary financial aid packaging, and other support services, including report writing, record keeping, accounting, and computer-related work. Peterson and others (1978) add that peer counselors could also provide walk-in counseling by maintaining office hours at various locations on campus, maintain a financial aid telephone hotline, provide outreach services, make "house calls" to student living units or other locations on a request basis, team-teach classes on financial aid programs and procedures, and under certain conditions even serve as residence hall financial aid counselors. The use of peer counselors in these and other ways could do much to relieve the professional counseling staff of all but the most critical or sensitive questions and decisions. The conclusions reached by McKenzie (1978) is accurate: professional financial aid counselors are spending too much time on duties and responsibilities of a paraprofessional nature.

Peer Counseling and the Revolving Door

While the point has been made that students are indeed a latent yet priceless asset to aid offices in a great many capacities, one area that has received little or no attention is counseling of aid recipients who are on scholastic probation. The remainder of this chapter describes a develmental framework for the setting up of a peer counseling program that addresses this need. The underlying framework comes from Peterson and others (1978), but the focus of the present model is assistance to academically deficient recipients of aid. Consequently, many features of the model developed in this chapter are specific rather than general, based as they are on the Student Facilitator Program of the Office of Student Financial Aid at the University of Texas at Austin.

Obviously, the dilemma of the revolving door is a common headache for financial aid administrators across the country. Countless low-income students enter college because of the availability of financial aid. However, many of these students drop out of college because of poor academic preparation, inadequate motivation, discrimination, or lack of financial resources (Pena and Vejil, 1976). While institutions must keep in mind that poverty and minority status are not necessarily synonymous, they must not remain blind to the fact that minorities are grossly over-represented among the nation's poor. Special efforts, including the targeting of peer counseling efforts to this population, may slow the revolving door and increase the retention of low-income and minority students—a federal mandate. The support and cooperation of the academic community is necessary to ensure the success of the program. Perhaps the impact of peer counseling services provided by the financial aid office may spark a drive to widen the scope of the program to other support services on campus.

Who Are the Financial Aid Recipients Who Are Not Making Satisfactory Progress? The financial aid staff must first examine the population of aid recipients who are not making satisfactory progress according to the policies of their institution, noting such factors as classification, ethnicity, sex, family income, grade point average, and major field of specialization. A summary of these data can provide insight into both problem sources and solutions. The data prove especially important when deciding who will have first priority in receiving counseling assistance, those with the lowest grade point average or those closest to the good-standing mark? Will graduate and professional students be assisted? Are academically deficient aid recipients concentrated in certain major areas, such as engineering or accounting? Will applicants for peer counselor positions be expected to have knowledge about and working experience with minority and low-income populations? Will graduate students be needed to counsel juniors and seniors?

Needless to say, an institution must have a genuine commitment to social change in order to meet the individual needs of its minority low-income students. The simplistic solution, of course, is to say that if standards, facilities, and services are uniform for all students, then everyone is being provided equal educational opportunity. This myopic response, however, is based on deficit theory and places all the responsibility for change on students. Fortunately, inequities such as these have been reconized and addressed by such recent legislation as Public Law 93-380, the Equal Educational Opportunities Act of 1974. Largely because of the laws and the courts, an increasing number of institutions are providing minority and low-income students with a greater variety of ancillary services and providing these services in a greater variety of ways.

What Support Services Exist on Campus? The second step is to determine the services and facilities that already exist to meet the needs of aid recipients on scholastic probation and to ascertain whether or not these services and facilities are being utilized by the target students. While the services and facilities provided vary with the sensitivity and genuine commitment of the individual institution, the following support services are required in some form to meet these students' needs: reading and study skills services, tutoring, personal counseling and psychological services, campus housing, career choice information, general libraries system, academic advising, financial aid, money management and community liaison services. While it is unrealistic to expect a financial aid office to provide paraprofessional counseling services in all these areas, there is a professional responsibility to know who is providing these services so that appropriate referrals can be made.

The variety of the support services needed is determined by the students themselves; rarely will an aid recipient be placed on scholastic probation as the result of a single factor. Peer counselors at the University of Texas (UT) at Austin found students' problems tended to develop in clusters until they manifested themselves in poor grades. Consequently, tutoring or study skills sessions were merely cosmetic solutions problems when true sources ran the gamut from family problems, poor self-concept, and inconsiderate roommates to being in the wrong major or working at several jobs because of poor money management skills or inaccurate financial aid information.

UT Austin is fortunate to have elaborate professional services in all these areas, yet when area directors were queried about the students who utilized their services, it was found that it was not the academically deficient recipients of aid who were making optimal use of the services and that the ongoing media blitz via the university radio and newspaper and campus bulletin boards had not been effective in motivating this particular target group to take advantage of the free services available on campus.

Is a Peer Counseling Program an Acceptable Alternative? The student financial aid office staff must decide whether to take counseling to students in the form of a peer counseling program. Traditionally, especially at large institutions, the response has been to let students sink or swim. But as administrators become more knowledgeable about and sensitive to the experiential backgrounds of minority and low-income students, increased personal contact services—whether supplied by professionals or paraprofessionals—are being called for in order to meet the need of these students. Obviously, the solution is nontraditional, because the students are nontraditional. Students' problems do not always surface during the professional counselors' structured eight-to-five workday. Moreover, some situations are best dealt with outside a formal office setting. Peer counselors live in the same setting, attend many of the same classes, and are usually in a better position than professional counselors to understand and address the students' problems. With such natural assets as credibility and empathy, well-informed, highly trained peer counselors have the advantage of being able to provide outreach and follow-up services that professional aid counselors cannot even hope to offer.

What Are the Specific Objectives of the Program? The needs, size, and commitment of the institution must be taken into consideration in establishing the specific objectives of the program. Clearly, there are two critical questions: Who is going to receive the services? What will the services provide? In determining who is to be served, it will first be necessary to review the federal regulations pertaining to student eligibility for financial assistance. There are two basic criteria concerning student status: that the student be enrolled in good standing as a regular student on at least a half-time basis and that the student be making satisfactory progress in his or her course of study. The regulations are complicated by the definition of good standing as the student's eligibility under the standards of the institution to continue in attendance. Satisfactory progress in the student's course of study as a criterion of student eligibility is not further defined in the regulations; it is, rather, the responsibility of the institution to make that definition. At UT Austin, for example, satisfactory progress is defined in the *General Information Bulletin* as follows: "Although a grade of D gives credit in a course, a minimum semester hour grade average of C is necessary for satisfactory progress towards a degree."

A literal interpretation would deny aid to all students with less than a 2.0 cumulative grade point average. In order to deal programmatically and humanely with the federal regulation in light of the institutional policy, the Financial Aid to Students Committee implemented the following policy on student eligibility for financial aid: If the 2.0 cumulative grade point average is not met once, a warning notice is mailed to the student or contact is made by a peer counselor; if the 2.0 cumulative grade point average is not met twice, no award is made for the subsequent award period; however, students who improve their academic status and who obtain a 2.0 cumulative grade point average again are eligible to receive aid.

Since continued scholastic probation does not necessarily provoke scholastic dismissal, the financial aid staff and committee members were concerned that disadvantaged students would face potential loss of financial assistance as the result of academic deficiency, while their more affluent colleagues would receive only a chiding letter from home. As a result, for the total population of aid recipients who were not making satisfactory progress and who risked loss of eligibility for financial aid, it was necessary to establish priorities for the peer counseling program based on the numbers involved and the availability of peer counseling staff. At UT Austin, priority has been assigned to minority and disadvantaged students and to first-time recipients (who in practice are freshmen and transfer students).

As for the second objective, the kinds of services that will be provided depend largely on the variety of services already available. Obviously, if central campus services in study skills, tutoring, and remedial reading do not exist, peer counselors may have to concentrate their energies on academic counseling in those skill areas. At institutions where a wide variety of student services is already available, paraprofessional assistance may take the form of facilitative, referral, and follow-up services, with the objective being to link the aid recipient with the appropriate services. In either case, the objective is distinctive in that the service is taken to the student not merely made available. A special, personal contact effort is made to maximize student participation over and beyond that motivated by the traditional open door student service.

From What Source Is Funding Available? An institution must provide or obtain the necessary funding and adequate physical facilities for the program. As with the UT Austin program, institutions may want to seek out soft monies that private foundations and corporations make available for experimental programs. The obvious advantage of such seed money is that an adequate program can be established within a short period of time without placing an undue fiscal burden on the operating budget of the student aid office. Further, the aid office has a distinct advantage in that its College Work-Study program can provide first choice on highly qualified peer counselors while at the same time helping the program stretch its budget dollars. Although the decision depends largely on the number of qualified applicants available through the work-study program, institutions must make every effort to hire the most highly qualified peer counselors available, even if it means that their salary or stipend must come entirely from the program's budget. Because of the extensive, highly sensitive counseling responsibilities of peer counselors, quality cannot be sacrificed to quantity.

Internships and practica are other options that aid offices can arrange with such departments as educational psychology, social work, or student personnel services, so that interns can receive academic credit in place of monetary compensation for serving as peer counselors. At UT Austin, the aid office screens interns in the peer counseling program and makes the final decision so as to avoid placements that would not be beneficial to the peer counseling program or to the intern involved. The drawback presented by internships is the turnover, as well as the need for training new interns every year.

What Are the Roles and Responsibilities of Peer Counselors? The individuals who develop the programs must clearly define the role of peer counselors and identify the responsibilities and activities to be undertaken by student paraprofessionals. Peer counselors who worked with academically deficient aid recipients are not misrepresented by their job title. Unlike other student employees classified as counselors as a result of substantial student contact or technical expertise, peer counselors use their extensive training in personal-crisis counseling as well as their broad knowledge base of university survival services to render ongoing assistance of a highly confidential nature to an assigned number of student clients. Because peer counselors place the counseling program as well as the entire financial aid office in a position of high exposure, one very critical implication of their highly visible public role is that their training must be extensive and intensive in applicable areas of technical and systemic procedures and especially in personal interaction skills.

While recognizing that peer counseling programs will vary significantly depending on the needs and resources of the individual institution, the duties and responsibilities of peer counselors nevertheless follow three basic service phases in assisting aid recipients on scholastic probation.

Initial Location and Contact Phase. Peer counselors can be assigned an equal number of student clients based on sex and class level. Peer counselors then make at least telephone contact (five documented attempts are recommended) with their assigned student clients. There is a dual purpose for this initial telephone contact: to ensure that student clients are aware of their probationary status and its effect on financial aid for subsequent semesters and to persuade the student client to meet personally with the peer counselor for an in-depth conference. The telephone contact has had a more positive effect on aid recipients at UT Austin than the customary warning letters to those who are placed on scholastic probation.

Personal Conference Phase. Peer counselors and student clients can meet at the financial aid office, in a dorm, the student center, or wherever the student client feels most comfortable. A great deal of information, such as the student client's major, housing status, high school, class, employment status, and so forth can be obtained by peer counselors from the financial aid files. The peer counselor should also have access to the student client's academic history records. Knowing the courses taken, the grades received, and the cumulative grade point average is extremely useful to the peer counselor in identifying certain patterns and problem areas. Prior to meeting with the student client, the peer counselor reviews the academic and financial aid information to anticipate problem areas to ask questions about and to consult with professional faculty or staff and validate the accuracy of policy information. Personal conferences with student clients should be diagnostic in nature. Utilizing appropriate interaction skills, peer counselors attempt to elicit information that might have a direct influence on the student client's academic performance. In the personal conference, the peer counselor should assist the student client to acknowledge that indeed there is a problem and to identify the nature of that problem.

Once the problem areas are identified, both the student client and the peer counselor can devise a plan of action, defining the student client's responsibilities in terms of self-help efforts. At this point, the peer counselor's responsibility is to provide the student client with accurate information about existing campus services that could provide assistance. This means that the peer counselor must have a thorough knowledge of such service areas as academic advising, tutoring, advanced placement testing, reading and study skills services, and counseling and psychological services. In cases where the student client is referred to a campus service, the first appointment can be set during the initial conference. The peer counselor has a list of contact persons who provide help in various areas, so the appointment can be made with a specific person. Preferably, this referral appointment takes place immediately after the initial conference.

Follow-Up Phase. At the conclusion of the initial conference, after alternatives have been identified, the peer counselor and the student client can agree on checkpoints for subsequent contacts. For the peer counselor, this may mean an evening phone call, a visit to the dorm, or a meeting for lunch. Depending on the situation, the peer advisor may be called on to contact professors, tutors, reading specialists, and others who may also be working with the student client to determine the student client's progress.

All this contact activity requires documentation. The peer counselor's administrative responsibilities consist of documenting all student client contacts. These confidential data can be recorded and filed in the peer counseling office (with photocopies of the information placed in the student client's financial aid folder). This documentation is critically important to the student client who is still not in good standing at the end of the grace semester, because financial aid review committees or similar bodies may look favorably at the student client's self-help efforts and feel authorized by the progress made or extenuating circumstances noted by the peer counselor to allow a second grace semester. Clearly, the peer counselor's recommendation is a significant factor in the committee's decision.

Who Will Supervise and Evaluate the Peer Counselors? Not only must the peer counselors' duties and responsibilities be clearly defined but formal and informal systems of reporting and supervision must be developed. The performance of duties can be evaluated directly by a program coordinator and communicated to peer counselors by means of periodic one-to-one conferences. Because of the flexible yet highly sensitive nature of the student client contacts, it is imperative that the program coordinator develop an effective system for monitoring progress reports submitted by peer counselors. In addition, weekly meetings of the coordinator with the peer counseling staff can be scheduled to discuss programmatic concerns, make overall progress and needs assessments, or discuss problem cases. An informal access system to the program coordinator's professional counseling assistance is essential for peer counselors. In the UT Austin program, the coordinator's office is adjacent to the peer counselors' office in order to facilitate access and supervision. Also, in addition to half-time financial aid duties, the program coordinator's job responsibilities stipulate that the coordinator is "on call" to assist peer counselors with highly sensitive cases or crises that occur throughout the day.

How Are Recruitment and Selection to Be Done? Two exacting aspects of a peer counseling program for academically deficient aid recipients are publicity and selection. Before the program can be publicized, however, it is important to develop materials containing an accurate job description, required and preferred eligibility criteria, and actual application forms. Required eligibility criteria may consist of a minimum number of semester hours earned; a minimum number of semesters of residency at the institution; a minimum cumulative grade point average; a minimum number of long semesters remaining to be earned; and demonstrable skills in communication, organization, and leadership. Preferred eligibility criteria may take the form of previous advisory experience with student populations; knowledge of such institutional policies and procedures as the adding or dropping of courses, the computation of grade point averages and scholastic probation; and knowledge of the institution's other student services, such as counseling and psychological services, reading and study skills services, and tutoring. In addition to such obvious media for publicity as newspapers, radio, and bulletin boards, job announcements and accompanying materials can be sent to deans, department chairpersons, faculty members, academic advisors, residence hall directors, student organizations (including those with large minority memberships), and the financial aid professional staff. Once the peer counseling program is established, experienced peer counselors can be asked to recommend potential applicants.

During the selection process, it is important to evaluate candidates on the basis of such critical variables as academic history and grade point average, study orientation, leadership experience, extracurricular involvement, personality characteristics, communication effectiveness, and peer acceptance. The first five attributes can be measured objectively, but the last three can only be assessed subjectively. It is easy to verify an applicant's grade point average from institutional records, but study orientation is more difficult to assess. Still, an instrument such as Brown's (1977) Effective Study Test can provide an accurate picture of an applicant's study skills. The leadership experience and extracurricular involvement listed on the application form by the potential peer counselor should receive special attention from the persons selecting peer counselors. Obviously, extracurricular activities reveal much about an applicant's strengths, skills, ambitions, and service attitudes. It is not so obvious, however, that extracurricular activities of economically disadvantaged applicants may be quite different from those of mainstream students. For example, mainstream applicants may be involved in campus organizations while economically disadvantaged students may have to hold several part-time jobs to make ends meet or to help with family expenses. Clearly, these activities reveal just as much about applicants' character as do more traditional ones, and should be considered equally significant in the selection process.

Good judgment and common sense, emotional stability, friendliness, tact, conversational effectiveness, and a sense of responsibility are personality characteristics that can be identified from letters of recommendation and in personal interviews. Questions testing applicants' strengths in these areas can be prepared in advance of the interview and asked of all applicants in order to evaluate the responses as fairly as possible. It is extremely important that those selected as peer counselors are representative of the target population to be served (not necessarily of the institution's general population) and that such critical factors as class, sex, ethnicity, and major area of specialization be considered.

Both the Process and Content of Training Are Important. Because the success or failure of the entire program rests principally on the strengths and weaknesses of the peer counselors, the training process has paramount importance. Because this paraprofessional program becomes a reflection of the aid office, the training component must be excellent. Clearly, those directly involved in training should be the best-qualified resource persons in the pertinent areas. Since peer counselors should be expected to be mini-experts on the campus services that might be of assistance to aid recipients, training should focus on such areas as interpersonal communication and crisis counseling; academic advising;

tutoring; reading, writing, and study skills improvement; the general libraries system; career choice information; money management; and financial aid. Lectures, demonstrations, discussions, role-playing activities, and on-the-job training can all be used, as appropriate, to assure that the requisite skills exist in all these baseline areas. In the UT Austin program, preservice on-site training is scheduled for each of the peer counselors on a rotating basis; this arrangement is ideal, because it provides hands-on experience for peer counselors and facilitates the formation of collegial relationships between peer counselors and contact persons in each of the campus service areas. Finally, time plays a critical role in the first phase of the program, since publicity, selection, and training should all take place before the initial school semester or session begins so that peer counselors can begin servicing students on the first day of classes.

Evaluation Must Be Planned in Advance. To determine the efficiency and effectiveness of a peer counseling program, a longitudinal evaluation design should be developed to examine the program from both product and process perspectives. Often, program evaluations are based solely on test scores, grade point averages or other product data. The inherent limitation of product data, however, is that they tell us only whether students are succeeding; they do not identify what is wrong with the process and what should be corrected. Hence, in addition to semester-end grade point average data comparing recipients of peer counseling assistance with nonparticipating students, a one-page, back-to-back questionnaire can be used to evaluate the program and the peer counselors. Such process evaluation can provide invaluable student client input that can be used for improving the program as well as each peer counselor's job performance.

The UT Austin program has received some very encouraging feedback from academically deficient aid recipients who received peer counseling assistance. During the first semester of program operation, for example, of the 316 aid recipients on scholastic probation, 48 percent decided to work with peer counselors. Seniors, generally presumed to be less likely to seek peer counseling assistance, had a surprisingly high rate of participation—51 percent. Minority students, presumed less likely to participate because of alienation, apathy, or both had as high as a 57 percent participation rate, whereas Anglo participants had a low of 38 percent. As for academic performance, of the 178 students who improved their grade point average, 52 percent received peer counseling assistance, 12 percent declined help, and 36 percent were never contacted because of inaccurate telephone number and address data. Thus, even if the program is viewed exclusively from a product perspective, it appears that students who work closely with peer counselors are more likely to improve their grade point average than students who do not.

The results of the program evaluation show that a great majority of survey respondents (75 percent) indicated that their initial reaction on finding out about peer counseling assistance was that "someone cared" about their plight. The high positive impression that "someone cared" reflected by Black and Chicano respondents (89 and 74 percent respectively) seems to indicate that this need is ethnically significant and that peer counselors address this need. As to the overall effectiveness of the program, UT Austin respondents felt that peer counselors helped them to improve their grades (59 percent), provided them with information that they were unaware of (76 percent), gave them enough tips to make conferences worthwhile (100 percent), and gave them hope and motivation to work harder (94 percent). In the area of new information, it should be noted that a very high percentage of Blacks and Chicanos (86 and 85 percent respectively) seemed to lack vital information concerning their academic problems. These findings seem to indicate that the traditional communications media are not reaching minority aid recipients as designed and that peer counselors can be vitally important sources of information. Finally, when asked if there existed a need for a peer counseling program at UT Austin, 100 percent of the respondents supported continuation of the program.

What About Student Responsibility?

In concluding, it would be naive to ignore critics who oppose "follow through" programs like this one because the programs baby students or because college students should be mature and responsible enough to succeed on their own. Our purpose here is not to deprecate opposing viewpoints but to describe a successful student assistance program based on the unique needs of academically deficient financial aid recipients. Clearly, the cornerstone of the program is the controversial posture of taking counseling services directly to the students who need them by means of student paraprofessionals. While peer counseling cannot be prescribed as a nostrum for the numerous problems that plague financial aid offices, there is ample evidence to support its use by aid offices wishing to meet increased administrative demands without sacrificing the all-important aspect of interpersonal counseling. The success of the UT Austin program supports the assertion that highly trained, properly supervised peer counselors can provide effective assistance to student peers in a highly professional manner. The procedure for setting up a peer counseling program described in this chapter is neither original nor immutable. Financial aid office staff wishing to explore the use of student paraprofessionals as peer counselors to meet the most critical needs of its own recipient population can also look to Brown (1977), Peterson and others (1978), and Delworth and Aulepp (1976). The uniqueness of the UT Austin program lies in the fact that it is one of the few programs, nationwide, that has been specifically designed to service academically deficient aid recipients who are in danger of losing their financial aid. At UT Austin, these often neglected students have had the experience of student-to-student counseling and found it to be very good indeed.

References

Brown, W. F. "Effectiveness of Paraprofessionals: The Evidence." *Personnel and Guidance Journal,* 1974, *53* (4), 257-263.

Brown, W. F. *Student-to-Student Counseling: An Approach to Academic Achievement.* Austin: University of Texas Press, 1977.

Brown, W. F., and others. "Effectiveness of Student-to-Student Counseling on the Academic Adjustment of Potential College Dropouts." *Journal of Education Psychology,* 1971, *62* (4), 285-289.

College Scholarship Service (CSS), Student Advisory Committee. *Unmet Needs: Report on Student Financial Aid Problems.* New York: College Entrance Examination Board, 1976.

Delworth, U., and Aulepp, L. *Training Manual for Paraprofessional and Allied Professional Programs.* Boulder, Colo.: Western Interstate Commission for Higher Education, 1976.

Education Amendments of 1976: Public Law 94-482. Sec. 493B, 90 Stat. 2149.

Equal Educational Opportunities Act of 1974: Public Law 93-380. Sec. 204, 20 U.S.C. Sec. 1703.

Johnson, R. W., and Frambs, G. "Financial Aid Office: Counseling and Outreach." *Journal of Student Financial Aid,* 1979, *9* (3), 28-34.

McKenzie, D. "Meeting the Consumerism Regulations: The Project at U. C. Berkeley." *Journal of Student Financial Aid,* 1978, *8* (2), 28-33.

National Center for Education Statistics (Fast Response Survey System). *Survey of Part-Time Student Financial Aid Counselors in Institutions of Higher Education.* Washington, D.C.: Office of Planning, Budgeting, and Evaluation, U.S. Office of Education, 1977.

National Student Educational Fund. *Who Are the Students Who Work in Campus Financial Aid Offices? A First Look.* Washington, D.C.: National Student Educational Fund, 1976.

Peña, R., and Vejil, E. "Financial Aid for Minority Students: Improving the Odds." *Journal of Student Financial Aid,* 1976, *6* (2), 4-8.

Pernal, M. "Efficiency and Accountability: A Computer-Assisted Financial Aid Operation for the Small College." *Journal of Student Financial Aid,* 1977, *8* (3), 35-42.

Stegura, D., and Olson, L. "Students Counsel Students in Financial Aid Offices." *The College Board Review,* 1977-78, Winter (106), 17-23.

U.S. Department of Health, Education, and Welfare. "How MISAA Will Affect Your Institution." *Bureau of Student Financial Aid Bulletin,* February 1979, p. 4.

U.S. Department of Health, Education, and Welfare. "Rules and Regulations (National Direct Student Loan, College Work-Study, Supplemental Educational Opportunity Grant Program." *Federal Register,* August 13, 1979, p. 47462.

Van Dusen, W. D., "The Coming Crises in Student Aid: Report on the 1978 Aspen Institute Conference on Student Aid Policy." *Journal of Student Financial Aid,* 1979, *9* (1), 3-18.

Jesús R. Gómez, former assistant director for student services, Office of Student Financial Aid, University of Texas at Austin, is director of the Student Financial Aid Office at Austin Community College, Austin, Texas.

Roberto Treviño-Martínez is a doctoral fellow in the College of Education, University of Texas at Austin. During the 1978-79 academic year, he served as counselor-coordinator of the Student Facilitator Program of UT Austin's Office of Student Financial Aid.

A decision to computerize the student financial aid office requires careful consideration and systematic evaluation of need. Potential users must consider the trade-offs between unfamiliar technology, specialization, and inflexibility and speed, accuracy, and control in attaining organizational goals and operational objectives.

Computerized Operations in Student Financial Aid: Relief or Restraint

Gordon E. Allen
James E. Zimmerman

The need for student financial assistance has grown rapidly in the past several years. Postsecondary educational institutions have seen as much as a threefold increase in the total aid dollars administered, and in some cases the number of students receiving aid has more than doubled. The Carnegie Council on Policy Studies in Higher Education (1979, p. 67) reports that appropriations for student financial aid have increased from $1.8 billion in 1974 to $4.9 billion in 1978. Commensurate with this growth, financial aid administration has been complicated by the creation of new aid programs, the refinement and regulation of existing programs, student demands for greater service, and institutional emphasis on recruiting efforts. While the demand for service in a number of areas within the institution has decreased and while institutions generally have felt a need to reduce the cost of service programs, the financial aid office has been growing and requiring a greater share of institutional resources.

In the face of a rapidly increasing workload, financial aid administrators have relied heavily on computers to do tasks traditionally accomplished by aid office staff. This reliance has introduced a new and complex technology for which financial aid administrators have not always been prepared. The purpose of this chapter is to explore the effects that computerization can have on the operation and organization of an office of student financial aid.

Facts About the Subject

In a study of the use of computers in financial aid office operations, Jepsen and Buchanan (1973) noted that financial aid administrators "who implemented a computer packaging system were satisfied that it helped them attain their goals and accomplish management objectives." Among the advantages of using a comprehensive computerized system were speed, time saving, accuracy, consistency in award making, and compliance with federal and institutional guidelines for use of funds. Other advantages mentioned by those interviewed were improved data and statistical analysis, simulation ability permitting evaluation of competing decision alternatives, and relief from purely clerical or mathematical functions.

The most frequently listed disadvantages of computerization were the necessity of coordination with and dependence on other campus offices, particularly the computer center; the potential loss of student record confidentiality; and the necessity of processing forms in bulk, which causes difficulty with some students.

In 1978, the Michigan Student Financial Aid Association (MSFAA), conducted a computerization study. The purpose of this study was to determine the extent to which institutions in Michigan were using computers to administer student financial aid. A survey form was developed to identify financial aid office functions supported by automatic data processing. The results of the survey are described below.

Conclusions

There is a wide range in the level of computer support for financial aid functions within the postsecondary institutions of Michigan. The responses provided by individuals who represented four-year public institutions seem to indicate that these schools, as a group, had the greatest level of computer utilization in general; however, it appears that there is not a high level of computer utilization to support the functions related to the administration of student financial aid. It was interesting to note that those functions which supported the business type operations within postsecondary institutions received the greatest level of support, while those functions that had the potential of providing the most direct service to students had the lowest level of support. For example, enrollment verification, creation of disbursement history, and the crediting of the student's account ranked first, second, and third with respect to level of support. Packaging (award determination), the printing of denial notices, and the tracking of application documents ranked fifteenth, sixteenth, and seventeenth. These three functions could have the greatest potential for improving direct service to students. Even though the use may not be intensive, the fact that the computer is being used in a variety of different ways to support the functions of financial aid suggests that a great deal of experience exists within the state. This fact creates a challenge for the Michigan Student Financial Aid Association (MSFAA). How can MSFAA foster the exchange of information that would facilitate the development of institutional systems in the future?" (*Utilization of Computers . . . ,* 1978)

Some attempts to computerize a financial aid office have failed miserably. Why? Wedemeyer (1978) points out some of the more significant reasons for failure, including the misconceptions that system develment will only take a few months, that one need only to "push the buttons" and the finished product will emerge, that activities will be greatly simplified, and that no additional staff will be necessary since the computer will do everything. In other words, the failure of attempts to computerize can often be traced to a lack of realism about computer development. Wedemeyer suggests that the lack of experience in data processing among financial aid officers is partly responsible. Expectations are often set too high and do not reflect realistic objectives.

According to Wedemeyer, factors which account for successful implementation of aid office data processing include a cooperative attitude from counseling-oriented financial aid staff members, receptive supervisors, a good rapport with the staff of the campus computer center, a distinct lack of fear of the computer, and confidence that a computer can be used to humanize the aid process. These issues will recur in the discussion of trade-offs.

The Systems Concept

One major reason for the failure of computer development projects is the lack of understanding and application of a systems concept by illustrating the components of a system: input, processing, and output. A distinction must be made between the data that require processing and the method that is used to process those data. The systems concept places the emphasis on the latter. Under the systems concept methodology, a group of data enters a predefined process which acts upon it, changes it, or creates new data from it.

Any considerations of computerizing all or part of the financial aid operation should include an examination of the entire financial aid process. As Rodgers (1978) points out, the integrated system is one that is partially or totally dependent on another system for the supply of data, and the financial aid operation is essentially a series of integrated systems.

The systems concept describes a methodology that helps people to order and structure complex problems. Buffa (1977) states that a systems methodology plots the relationships and interactions of various elements affecting the problem or procedure being examined. This methodology helps us to understand the problem and provide for its solution. One important assumption of the system concept is that a system is defined not so much by the components themselves as by the unique combination of components that make up the whole. This is precisely the point made by Rodgers in his description of integrated systems and it will be examined again in the discussion of trade-offs. Here, it suffices to say that a decision to computerize should start with a complete examination of the operating system.

Trade-Offs

It can be safely assumed that to introduce computerization into the financial aid office is to add technology to the organization. There are varying opinions on the effects of technology on an organization. Woodward (1970) was one of the first to discover that the introduction of technology into an operation had significant effects on the attitudes of employees. They developed a feeling that the system was dictating the performance of their jobs, not their own initiative, and alienation and a sense of the loss of individual freedom were the results. This problem can occur in a computerized financial aid office. Employees may not use the system as it was designed to be used, or they may not use the system at all. In extreme cases, an employee may even sabotage the system to regain his individual identity. Financial aid administrators are familiar with inflexible regulations and procedures, and introduction of such a new technology as the computerized system may cause feelings of alienation that had already existed but had not been expressed.

The financial aid office is a combination of many technologies — administrative, economic, and social. Dewar and Hage (1978) point out that different technologies require different kinds of management expertise and specialized occupations. In addition, the more complex the technology, the greater the need for these new occupational specialists. As a result, the financial aid administrator may face one of two problems: an inability to obtain or gain access to occupational specialists, which limits the growth potential within that technology, or, if indeed, the occupational specialists are available, the financial aid administrator may not have the technological expertise to express his needs coherently to them.

Nevertheless, the financial aid administrator is likely to seek to add these specialists to his staff, and, as a result, the operation will increase in technological complexity. It is not clear, according to Dewar and Hage, that size and complexity are directly related. However, one rule of thumb is that the higher the complexity, the higher the level of average training received by employees and the fewer the personnel who can be substituted in a given task without the need for extensive retraining. Add to this the complicating characteristics of seasonal operations and dependence on agencies outside the control of the financial aid office and the result is a very real danger of severe backlogs and confusion with no adequately trained personnel to help. Such routine occurrences as employee turnover, policy changes, and budget limitations can be the final blow and render the financial aid administrator helpless in his attempt to meet the objectives of timely delivery, accuracy, and compliance with financial aid program requirements.

Inflexibility is frequently identified as one trade-off in computerized operations. This inflexibility is frequently generated by a failure to use a systems approach to computerization. Such critical decisions as what data are needed, how the data will be accessed, and the equipment, personnel, and policies that are required to support these needs are often made in haste. At least one cause of this haste is the usual problem of communication between user and specialist.

This idea of hasty decision making is easily related to the "halo error," a term used in appraisal of personnel performance. Flippo (1976, p. 274-275) describes this error as a decision made on the basis of one aspect of "a person's character or performance" rather than on consideration of all aspects of a person's performance. "No person is likely to be perfectly good or perfectly bad; one is generally better in some areas than in others." This idea is easily transferred to decisions involving computerized systems. In the systems concept, the entire system is reviewed for the purpose of identifying weaknesses and strengths in the operating system. To complete the analogy, we could say no system is likely to be perfectly good or perfectly bad; the system is generally better in some areas than in others. It is therefore necessary to identify the points at which weaknesses exist before consideration of mechanization is addressed.

Consider the following hypothetical example: The financial aid administrator at Yourtown University, U.S.A., has recently returned from a professional workshop where he witnessed a demonstration of an on-line financial aid system; that is, a system in which data is entered directly into the computer from terminals. He had encountered the term before, and he had heard fellow financial aid administrators talking about on-line processing, but this presentation had convinced him that on-line processing was just what he needed. Besides, other offices on his campus already had this capability and he was certain that he could convince his administration to allow his office to take advantage of it, too.

Many weeks later, after considerable discussion and justification, the request for a terminal and programming support is approved and a systems analyst is assigned to the project. Although the financial aid administrator is pleased with the progress of this request, a new operating cycle is under way in his office and time has become critical. At the first meeting of the systems analyst and the financial aid administrator the financial aid administrator makes an effort to help the analyst to become familiar with the current system and its exact needs. Many weeks go by and the analyst continues to ask questions, many times over the telephone, until the system implementation is finally complete.

The first year in which on-line processing is used is a little rough, because of the usual problems accompanying a system change of this kind, but, all in all, the financial aid administrator is pleased, and the operating cycle is completed with some expectations met.

At the start of the second year, the financial aid administrator is again deeply involved in a new operating cycle. A request is made to data processing for "slight" changes in some of the programs, but the response is that priority is being given to other major changes and that the request will have to wait. The assistant director has asked for advice on problems involving the terminal. Backlogs of information to be entered continue to build up. Terminal operators are part-time because of budget limitations. The turnover among operators has created severe training and scheduling problems. When the computer system goes down, processing comes to a standstill. Counselors are continually going through the paper around the terminal in an effort to determine the status of changes they have made, and this activity interrupts the operators. Several unusual errors have been discovered, and it is suspected that either the operators are not entering information correctly or that the programs are not calculating the data correctly. The assistant director states that the only solution is to purchase two more terminals, hire three full-time employees to operate them, and create a batch system to back up the on-line system. The assistant director adds that the slow response time on the terminals alone is causing a loss of valuable time. At this point, the financial aid administrator feels frustrated and wonders what can be done after so much time and money has already been invested. Is the answer still more?

This hypothetical situation not only demonstrates the inflexibility of some computerized operations but it also suggests that the financial aid administrator usually does not have the choice of abandoning the technology for the sake of flexibility.

There are many reasons why this situation can occur. The systems analyst could have provided clearer alternatives. The financial aid administrator could have considered each decision more carefully. However, a more basic error is the failure to review the operating system being computerized. Was on-line processing indeed the improvement that was needed? Did it strengthen the overall system and eliminate most of the weak points in processing?

In the preceding discussion of occupational specialists, one point that was not mentioned was the effect of computer technology on organizational patterns or designs. Ford and Slocum (1977) summarize the available research on this issue. First, it is agreed that technology affects organizational structure. The precise impact is not certain, but there is some indication that organizational change is related to the number of different technologies involved. Second, the impact of technology is likely to be selective, affecting certain parts of the organization and not affecting others. Third, most research suggests that organizational effects are not so much a function of technology itself as the dependency of an organization on technology. To illustrate the effects of computerization on a financial aid office, consider the example of the University of Texas (UT) at Austin.

UT Austin is a large, multilevel, state-supported institution, that has 45,000 undergraduate, graduate, and professional students enrolled on one campus. The financial aid office utilizes approximately fifty full-time employees, and all major areas have been computerized. The organizational structure of this office distinguishes two major functional divisions: operations and student services. Within the operations division there are three sections: data processing, financial aid, and accounting. The student services division is composed of four sections: counseling, information dissemination, student employment, and special programs. Each of the seven sections is supervised by an occupational specialist, a systems analyst, a specialist in financial aid programs and regulations, an accountant, a specialist in professional writing and information systems, a personnel specialist, and a specialist in culturally and economically disadvantaged students. Each of these individuals has unique qualifications in education and experience.

This specialization pattern of the organizational structure at UT Austin represents a reaction to technology as it was introduced in various areas over the past several years. The introduction of computerized payment procedures within this office caused the needs of that specialized function to stand out from those of other work functions. It was therefore fairly easy to organize that group under one supervisor. With the increase in the use of the computer and related activities, it was easy to identify a group of primarily data processing functions, which could also be organized into a group under one supervisor. As computer technology was added, this growth pattern continued, until most of the purely operational functions had been computerized and organized as separate groups under individual supervisors. Once the growth pattern had reached this point, it became easy to distinguish the operating functions from the counseling and student service functions. In addition, since most of the clerical functions were centralized in the operations division, more time became available for counseling, liaison, and other student service functions. It was therefore easy to identify these three activities as specialized functions and to place one supervisor over those performing each. The organizational pattern at UT Austin may not be the best organizational pattern for every financial aid office, and its development may only have partially been the result of increasing technology, but it does illustrate the impact that computer technology can have as a growth pattern occurring over time.

The Alternatives

What are the alternatives facing the financial aid administrator when the decision to computerize is being considered? The first step is to examine the decision itself. Is computerization a viable option? If so, is the time right and are the necessary resources available? If the answers are yes, how much of the operating system would be improved under computerization? More generally, how much better will the use of the computers enable the financial aid administrator to realize organizational goals and objectives? Are the resources required for computerization better allocated elsewhere? What are the advantages and disadvantages? Answers to such preliminary questions are crucial to decisions that are often assumed to be unimportant, unrelated, or correct without examination. In short, is there a substantial need for computerization or is it merely an attempt to get on the bandwagon?

One alternative in computerization of the financial aid operation is purchase of the required technology by hiring outside specialists to evaluate and recommend the particular computer application that is required. This usually takes less time than internal development. The purchase of technology from an outside supplier, however, warrants careful study. Regulations governing student financial aid allow aid administrators considerable flexibility in determining award eligibility and in the packaging of individual students. As a result of this flexibility, institutions have developed unique philosophies and procedures. These characteristics reflect and support institutional goals and objectives. Utilization of an outside product may require changes at odds with the institution's student aid philosophy and procedures.

If the supplier is able to adjust to the unique needs of individual offices, a second point becomes critical. With changing regulations, different philosophies and procedures, conflicting institutional priorities, and changing technology, who is to maintain the computer system over time? How long will this maintenance be available, and how quickly can changes be accomplished? Is the available technology cost-efficient if it also serves other priorities?

These considerations resemble those involved in the lease or purchase of large capital improvements. If needs and institutional priorities are tentative or short-term and if the institutional environment is one of change, the financial aid administrator may want to seek outside technology as a short-term solution. The resources required would represent the expense of doing business in a changing environment. However, if long-range institutional priorities are clearly defined and major operating systems are well established, the best strategy may be to use outside technology as a permanent solution to system needs. This option may be ideal for smaller institutions with little or no access to a computer or even for larger institutions with inadequate computer support.

Whatever the size of the institution, another alternative is to develop computer support from within. This approach is usually more difficult than the alternative of purchasing outside technology and is frequently associated with larger institutions that have considerable computer resources. As previously pointed out, greater reliance upon computers means greater reliance on people with computer experience; that is, on systems analysts and computer programmers. These specialists are usually in high demand within a given institution, and their work assignments reflect institutional priorities. Institutions may be reluctant to commit analysts and programmers to a student financial aid office. At some institutions, the administrator may have the flexibility to create a permanent staff position for a data processing person. By creating such a staff position, the financial aid administrator avoids the vulnerability of changing institutional priorities and is reasonably assured of continued support.

In financial aid offices that have limited access to computer support because of high demand on the computer center by other offices, the financial aid administrator may have to wait in line to gain access. Pernal (1977) thinks that this may not be entirely bad, since, in effect, waiting in line is a rationing technique, which prevents the "do everything" approach to development; that is, the person who waits in line is forced to consider only the absolutely essential needs.

Internal development of the required technology will require careful consideration of the environment in which the financial aid administrator is working. Systems development may be considered in terms of evolution versus revolution. System development in which additional features are added to a core or basic system as needed is evolutional development. The system grows or evolves as office functions are computerized. System revolution occurs when an attempt is made to change or redesign all data processing support completely. Generally, institutions are better prepared to provide and accept evolving systems support. The aid administrator identifies a modification or enhancement to the existing system, and the data processing center assigns the work. Relatively few systems resources are needed, and their commitment is for comparatively short periods of time. Complete redesign of an existing system or design of a sophisticated, comprehensive system may require a commitment exceeding institutional capabilities.

Additional factors contributing to an aid administrator's decision to computerize depend on the data processing environment at the institution. The environment may be such that the aid administrator can proceed with systems development as he chooses. This situation occurs in a decentralized environment in which the data processing office provides technical support and advanced systems support and the user office provides its own program maintenance and system modification.

However, other institutions take a more centralized approach to systems development, and since the centralized approach is the more common of the two, the following example should be helpful. The University of Michigan provides centralized administrative data processing support to user departments. To ensure overall systems continuity and to provide systems users and prospective users with data processing systems development instructions, the University's Office of Administrative Systems (1980) has published a *Project Management Guide*. This guide describes the university's seven-phase project development cycle, including committee responsibility and composition, and it well illustrates the centralized data processing environment. The following is a summary of the seven phases described in the guide.

Phase I: Project Initiation. This phase provides a mechanism for requesting services from the Office of Administrative Systems, specifies the content of such requests, and describes the procedures for completing this phase of the project development cycle.

Phase II: Project Definition. The purpose of this phase is to define the scope, objectives, and control mechanisms of the proposed system. Relationships to and interactions with other current and future systems are identified in order to determine the overall impact of the proposed system. Preliminary cost-benefit and time estimates are developed, and structured analysis concepts are introduced. At the end of this phase, the information that has been developed is documented in a Project Definition Report.

Phase III: General Systems Design. The purpose of this phase is to describe in greater detail what the system is intended to accomplish. Method-of-operation charts begun in the previous phase are expanded with additional detail. Organizational controls are determined, the time requirements for data are analyzed, the required data elements are identified, and basic data base relationships are established. Cost estimates are revised, and planning for later development phases is begun. The results of these design activities are documented in a General Systems Design Specification.

Phase IV: Detail Systems Design. In this phase, the focus of activity shifts to the technical aspects of systems development—how rather than what. Structured design charts are developed down to the program level. Input/output transaction definitions, data element definitions, and individual program specifications are completed. The Systems Journal, Program Folders, and User's Operations Guide are begun. Estimated cost and time requirements of project development are refined, and planning for the remaining phases of the project is completed. The results of this activity are summarized in the Detail Systems Design Summary. If the project is to be divided into several stages, a Detail Systems Design Summary is normally prepared for each stage.

Phase V: Programming and Testing. This phase of the project consists of the design, coding, testing, debugging, and documenting of the program, subroutines, and system specified in the preceding phase. System and user documentation was also developed during the preceding phase. In this phase, system performance is assessed during testing, and changes in the system design are made as required, using the approved change procedure. Management approvals are acquired, including written user acceptance. The results of these activities are recorded and stored in Program Folders, Job Folders, and System Journals, according to certain standards. At the end of this phase, the complete system is ready for installation.

Phase VI: Systems Installation. The objectives of this phase are to convert the current operation to the new system in accordance with the conversion plans developed during the Detail Systems Design phase and to replace the current process with the new system. At the completion of this phase, the system should be operating in a normal production environment.

Phase VII: Systems Review. A review of the course of project development provides information that can be used to improve the development process in future projects and to identify where changes or enhancements in the completed system may be required. For multiphased development projects, the Systems Review may occur after each phase or after several phases and at the completion of the final phase, as determined by the Office of Administrative Systems project manager.

At the end of this phase, the Project Review document is produced for management review.

Progress from the project initiation phase to the systems review phase is controlled by requirements for securing committee approval and signature on all required system documentation (Project Definition, General System Design Specification, Detail Systems Design Summary, and so forth). The Project Management Guide identifies committee composition and responsibility to ensure intrauniversity systems continuity and compatibility. This use of committees that follow a predefined guide for systems development at multiple levels of the organization is a good example of the centralized approach.

It is important to emphasize user involvement. The user, in this case the financial aid administrator, is the principal representative of the department being computerized and as such has a critical role in the decision-making process.

Conclusion

The decision to computerize a financial aid office requires careful consideration. It involves the use of considerable resources and greatly alters the service provided by a financial aid office. It requires an informed decision maker who realizes the impact of introducing a new technology into the organization. The public relations implications are important, particularly as they affect prospective aid applicants and high school personnel. There is the danger of making such dramatic changes that the staff may be lost in a complex system it cannot operate. It is necessary to establish the specific objectives that are to be accomplished with the computer. These objectives should come from a review of the whole operating system. Priorities should be established for the computerization of various parts of the existing system, and a procedure for continuously monitoring computer systems in use should be developed. It is likely that this procedure will create a need for new staff, more specialized staff, new organizational structures, and an avoidance of the one-time-shot attitude.

Finally, Wedemeyer makes the point that the staff must believe that the financial aid office can become more humanized if computerized operations are added. A financial aid counselor cannot counsel a student on financial decisions if he is so overwhelmed by paperwork that he does not have the time. Used within its proper design, a computer can contribute heavily to an environment characterized by professionally oriented counselors and more informed managers using a generally more creative approach to provide more effective services to students.

References

Buffa, E. S. *Modern Production Management.* (5th ed.) New York: Wiley, 1977.
Carnegie Council on Policy Studies in Higher Education. *Next Steps for the 1980s in Student Financial Aid: A Fourth Alternative.* San Francisco: Jossey-Bass, 1979.
Dewar, R., and Hage, J. "Size, Technology, Complexity, and Structural Differentiation: Toward a Theoretical Synthesis." *Administrative Science Quarterly,* 1978, *23* (1), 111-118.
Flippo, E. B. *Principles of Personnel Management.* New York: McGraw-Hill, 1976.
Ford, J. D., and Slocum, J. W., Jr. "Size, Technology, Environment, and Structure of Organizations." *The Academy of Management Review,* 1977, *2* (4), 561-570.
Jepsen, K. J., and Buchanan, T. M. "Financial Aid Decisions Made by Computer." *College Management,* 1973, *8* (8), 17-18.
Office of Administrative Systems. *Project Management Guide.* (4th ed.) Ann Arbor: Office of Administrative Systems, University of Michigan, 1980.
Pernal, M. "Efficiency and Accountability: A Computer-Assisted Financial Aid Operation for the Small College." *Journal of Student Financial Aid,* 1977, *7* (3), 47-49.
Rodgers, W. *Topics in Financial Aid: Data Management.* Iowa City, Iowa: American College Testing Program, 1978.
"The Utilization of Computers to Support the Administration of Financial Aid in Post-Secondary Institutions in Michigan." Unpublished report of MSFAA Data Processing Committee. Fall 1978.
Wedemeyer, R. H. "Computerizing Student Financial Aid." *Journal of Student Financial Aid,* 1978, *8* (1), 23-24.
Woodward, J. *Industrial Organization: Behavior and Control.* Oxford, England: Claredon Press, 1970.

As assistant director of the Office of Student Financial Aid at the University of Texas at Austin, Gordon E. Allen is the primary designer and coordinator of automated systems. He has served as trainer and consultant on computerized systems for local, regional, and national institutions and agencies.

As associate director of the Office of Financial Aid at the University of Michigan, James E. Zimmerman is the primary designer and coordinator of automated systems. He has served as trainer and consultant on computerized systems for local, regional, and national institutions and agencies and written several articles on the subject.

The unprecedented growth and complexity of financial assistance programs have increased the necessity for administrators of college and university student financial aid offices to possess management skills so that those offices can be integrated into institutional plans and priorities.

The Application of Open System Theory to Student Financial Aid Administration

Shirley F. Binder

There can be no more rewarding, exciting, frustrating, or demanding profession than student financial aid administration. It is a developing profession. According to Parish (1975, p. 54), "The title 'Financial Aid Officer' is one relatively new to the academic community, and the job description of those who currently bear the title hardly existed prior to the 1950s." There is no recognized formal academic training prescribed for aid administrators. As reported in a survey of the profession made in 1974 and again 1977 by the National Association of Student Financial Aid Administrators (NASFAA) (1978, p. viii), "The master's degree, if not a formal requirement for a financial aid director, was an informal one. Of those responding, over 60 percent had a master's or higher degree. A financial aid director with a doctorate remained a rarity."

The NASFAA survey found, further, that there was "considerable difference between the academic courses thought 'useful' and the ones the financial aid directors had taken themselves. Of the courses listed in the 1974 survey, only counseling had been taken by the majority of financial aid directors." In a similar survey conducted in 1979, John Garlock (1980, p. 142) indentified accounting and statistics as a course of study frequently found in the educational background of financial aid directors in the Southwest.

The dramatic growth in the size and complexity of financial assistance programs over the last decade has placed tremendous demands on financial aid directors and on their institutional executive officers to ensure effective administration of these programs. One recent publication directed to university presidents (El-Khawas, 1979, p. 3) identifies the requirements of this expanding administrative burden as: "development of new administrative procedures; rapid adjustment to changing demands, funding levels, and staffing needs; close attention to federal regulations; growing responsibilities for cash management and loan collection; and greater risk of financial dislocation if funding levels change or enrollment projections are wrong."

However, financial aid directors are not the only college and university administrators with little formal training for their job. According to Gaff and others (1978, p. 88), "Most college and university administrators have not been trained in the skills demanded of them as educational executives; they have neither planned for careers in administration nor studied others functioning successfully in similar roles." Walter Bennis, an authority on organizational development is quoted: "Although . . . academic administrators acquire skills in various ways both before and after assuming administrative positions, little of that development comes from systematic or inservice training." Gaff and others are writing of deans, department chairmen, and other academic administrators; however, the same is true of financial aid directors.

In the competition among administrative units for personnel, space, data processing support, and so forth, student financial aid directors have operated at a disadvantage. Although their administrative training and experience is probably no better or no worse than those of other university administrators, in most cases they have not gained the stature and support they felt was deserved or necessary. The reasons are varied. Growth in the programs has resulted in a continuing need for more space, personnel, and equipment. The lack of academic credentials and research skills shared by most aid administrators may have blocked their acceptance by faculty and student affairs staff at some colleges and universities. The aid director is a new administrator on campus, representing a service that did not exist during the undergraduate and even graduate study of many of his faculty and staff colleagues. Finally, the involvement of the student financial aid administrator in regulatory processes surrounding the federal financial assistance programs has been viewed by some executive officers as an attempt at policymaking, which is a presidential responsibility.

Nevertheless, financial aid administrators have a unique opportunity to serve as change agents on university campuses. Effective administration of financial assistance programs can result in dramatic shifts in the size, age, ethnic, and socioeconomic mix of the student body. Policies relating to refunds of student charges; to timing, clarity, and coordination of information disseminated to students; and to efforts made in support of student persistence have all been influenced by the regulations applicable to Title IV federal student assistance programs.

Effective administration of financial aid programs for students is the result of a systematic and comprehensive plan for those services. The financial aid administrator must be a manager, develop a management style, and approach the administration of aid programs with some understanding of planning or management theory. One approach to planning is the open systems theory described by Edwin Bell (1978, pp. 12–15). According to Bell, there are eight basic concepts in the open system theory:

1. The systems are by definition open; that is, they cannot survive in isolation from other various environments.
2. Any organization or any part of an organization should be viewed as a system within a system.
3. The same final state can be reached from different initial positions and in different ways; that is, open systems operate on the principle of equafinality.
4. An open system has a purpose and uses complex feedback and regulatory mechanisms to adapt to environmental change and to see whether its own environmental manipulations have been effective.
5. Organizations, within this perspective, are viewed as patterned sets of events. In other words, the organization is what it does, not what its situation says it is.

6. Organizations have boundaries that vary in permeability and location according to the transactions involved and the issues under consideration.
7. The interaction in the system reflects different layers of control and autonomy. Some subsystems have varying degrees of power over other subsystems.
8. Open system theory is not reductionist. It does not try and break things down to their lowest common denominator but tries to provide perspective . . . .

These eight concepts can be applied to the administration of a student financial aid office and to integration of that service into the total services available to students on the campus. Following are some practical applications of open systems theory to management of an aid office and to integration of aid programs into institutional plans and priorities.

"The systems are by definition open: that is, they cannot survive in isolation from other various environments" (Bell, 1978, p. 12).

The environments that are relevant to student financial aid administration are both internal (campus) and external (federal and state government, private donors). In regard to the internal environment, student financial aid administrators must realize that satisfactory progress policies for financial aid recipients may be challenged by faculty in the face of declining enrollments; that coordination of aid on campus to prevent overawards can be viewed by some as "control"; that subgroups of students, supported by faculty, staff, and in the case of public institutions by state legislators as well, may seek special consideration for expeditious attention to their applications or for award of preferred forms of assistance (grants and scholarships rather than loans and work programs); and that faculty and other staff may view a College Work-Study program that pays 80 percent of the student's wages as a supplement to their own financial resources. As for external environments, precipitous changes in regulations can result in unplanned and immediate need for additional staff to perform newly required functions; anticipated program funding can be delayed or curtailed as the result of state or federal action or inaction; and late receipt of notification of allocations of federal funds results in delayed packaging of aid, award notification to students, and enrollment.

The effect of contradictory internal policies and practices, of positive or negative changes in funding levels, and of new federal regulations must be anticipated and communicated to the appropriate officials within the institution. Well-established and well-communicated policies and procedures and the guarantee of due process ensured by a published appeal process will provide relief from internal pressures. Short-term solutions to added responsibilities resulting from changes in the external environment such as temporary staff assignments, are generally more available than permanent staff additions and can allow thoughtful consideration of appropriate long-range solutions as well as provide immediate relief to frustrated students and burned out staff. Further, as anyone who has served in financial aid administration can attest, the difficult situation created by a given set of regulations can be replaced by a different, albeit equally difficult, situation through a Notice of Proposed Rule Making and subsequent interim, revised, and final regulations. The speed with which these changes occur is such that, on occasion, the United States Government Printing Office has been incapable of providing a printed copy of the regulations before the deadline established for public comment has passed, which in turn results in an extension of the deadline and communication of that fact to all participating institutions.

Thus, although it is important to provide an accurate flow of information to higher administrative levels as well as within the particular subsystem, it is also vital that that information be tempered when it relates to potential changes as they appear in proposed regulations. Of course, this is, indeed, the time to express institutional and individual opinion to the Office of Education on proposed changes but it may also be premature to request budget increases for the subsystem to accommodate requirements that are still in the proposal stage. It is not, however, premature to develop a plan of action and to communicate that plan to the next administrative level.

"Any organization or any part of an organization should be viewed as a system within a system" (Bell, 1978, p. 12).

By definition, the student financial aid office is a subsystem of the college or university. Each of the subsystems of the university has unique needs and problems to face. Each must recognize the needs and problems of other subsystems in relation to the mission of the institution. Even during the most favorable times, when enrollments were increasing at a steady and predictable rate and inflation and power shortages and tax revolts had yet to cast a mood of impending disaster over higher education, all the needs of all the subsystems of an institution could not be met at the time when they were requested. In the present economic climate, when the very survival of some institutions is at stake, decisions regarding budget increases for various subsystems will be based on the income potential of the subsystem or on its impact on student enrollment and tuition income. In order to clearly establish the budget and resource needs of the student financial aid office, the administrator must identify the relationship between the service that will be provided or improved and institutional enrollment.

A detailed analysis of the services provided by the subsystem may be required by the financial aid administrator in determining the budget and resources requirements. However, to ensure that the financial aid office request can compete with the requests from other subsystems, the financial aid administrator must summarize the data, present clear evidence of need based on empirical data, and make an honest request for resource allocation. At times, these needs will not be met. Services provided by the subsystem must then be reassessed, and curtailment of services or procedural revisions resulting from budget cuts or lack of increase must be communicated to the next administrative level. The effective administrator will acknowledge evidence of greater need by other subsystems when it is presented and build bridges of support for future needs from the administrators of other subsystems by such acknowledgment. This presupposes a free flow of information within the system and a great deal of interaction between both individuals and groups. It further assumes "a flow of information down, up, and among peers; general acceptance of communication from above and accurate flow of communication from below; and generally open and candid questioning" (Eble, 1978, pp. 41-42).

"The same final state can be reached from different initial positions and in different ways; that is, open systems operate on the principle of equifinality" (Bell, 1978, p. 12)

The changes brought about by the external environment, over which the student financial aid administrator has little or no control, place additional burdens on that office although, as stated earlier, the institution may fail to respond with additional resources. In that event, the administrator must reexamine the services provided by the subsystem and ask the following questions: What functions are required of the office by statute and governmental regulation, by institutional policy, and by good administrative practice? What functions are now being performed by this office? What functions could be eliminated or curtailed? What functions could be transferred to another subsystem? What functions currently performed manually could be machine processed?

As requirements change, services and procedures must be reassessed in light of the goals of the system. Although change as such is neither positive nor negative, flexibility, resiliency, and a willingness on the part of the administrator to meet challenges are required to anticipate the problems created by change. Involving other subsystems by a request for shared responsibility can create system-wide awareness of the complexities involved in student assistance programs.

"An open system has a purpose and uses complex feedback and regulatory mechanisms to adapt to environmental change and to see whether its own environmental manipulations have been effective" (Bell, 1978, p. 13).

The National Association of Student Financial Aid Administrators offers a Guide to Institutional Self-Evaluation, which, if it is used annually to assess procedures and policies employed in the financial aid office, will identify areas of noncompliance with federal regulations and established practice. Required nonfederal compliance audits reflect the relative soundness of accounting procedures. The default rate on student loans processed by the aid office is an indicator of the due diligence with which collection efforts are made by or for the institution. Finally perceptions of students, faculty, and staff at the institution serve to point out strengths and weaknesses in the operation.

To be effective, evaluation must be ongoing and changes must be made if they are indicated. Evaluation is time-consuming and sometimes painful, it is also an integral step in the application of a system approach to management.

"Organizations, within this perspective, are viewed as patterned sets of events. In other words, the organization is what it does, not what its situation says it is" (Bell, 1978, p. 13).

According to federal policy, the role of student financial assistance is to enable access, choice, and persistence of needy students in postsecondary education. If, in fact, the policies of the institution or of the financial aid office itself produce an apparent lack of sensitivity to the total needs of disadvantaged students, the financial assistance programs at that institution may be viewed as obstructive rather than facilitative. Some examples: failure to provide linkages for disadvantaged students to campus and community helping resources; eight-to-five office hours at a college that traditionally enrolls a high percentage of part-time students who are also full-time employees; staff members who are unavailable or unwilling to meet with students and discuss their problems; impersonal identification of students by number, rather than by name; lack of an appeal process for use by students who do not feel they have received a fair hearing of their problem or complaint.

Responsibility for providing or revising services and procedures to facilitate access, choice, and retention of disadvantaged students is not necessarily in the purview of the financial aid administrator. However, it is the administrator's responsibility, at the very least, to sensitize financial aid office staff to these needs to make the stated and the perceived purposes of that office congruent.

"Organizations have boundaries that vary in permeability and location according to the transactions involved and the issues under consideration" (Bell, 1978, p. 13).

Good internal control requires separation of the awarding and disbursing functions of the student financial aid office. However, it is in the best interest of student clients that the two offices responsible for these functions not only be close physically but also philosophically. In other words, the cashier in the bursar's office who hands the student an aid check is seen by the student as part of the financial aid operation. Close communication between offices and a shared philosophy of student services or a shared fiscal approach reinforce student perceptions of the aid office, whether that perception is positive or negative.

"The interaction in the system reflects different layers of control and autonomy. Some subsystems have varying degrees of power over other subsystems" (Bell, 1978, p. 13).

In a complex and decentralized university there are many examples of this characteristic of open systems that presents a potential for conflict. Colleges and departments of such universities may control funds from private endowments, research grants, and foundations that provide scholarships for students enrolled in those units. Federal regulation requires monitoring of all financial assistance available on campus in order to prevent the award of federal funds which, when combined with other assistance, result in awards in excess of documented need. Although federal regulations place power over the academic units and affected students in the hands of the financial aid administrator, use of that power through threat of federal sanction will not build bridges between the academic and student services subsystems. Rather, negotiation and agreement on principle, followed by procedural linkages, will allay fears of federal infringement and involve the academic subsystems in the financial aid process.

Other examples include the power of the accounting department over the financial aid office created by its production of checks and of the data processing office over both through the programming support that it provides. The larger the institution, the more important it becomes for administrators of subsystems in general and for the student financial aid office in particular to know the personnel in other units who are responsible for getting the job done and to work cooperatively with them.

"*Open system theory is not reductionist. It does not try and break things down to their lowest common denominator but tries to provide perspective . . .*" (Bell, 1978, p. 13).

An effective office of student financial aid does more than process applications, identify eligibility for programs and dollar amounts, disburse funds, and report expenditures in the following year's application for funds. It is, or it should be, the campus control point and referral agency for all the helping services that may be required by students and their families with a documented or felt financial need. Counseling, referring, advising, and teaching are as much a part of financial aid as auditing, data processing, accounting, and loan collection.

Another contributing factor is the level of risk taking. Again, as anyone involved in student financial aid can attest, there is a little of the Mississippi River boat gambler in the effective aid administrator. Risks on individual students are everyday affairs; an aid administrator may have to decide to approve a loan of several thousand dollars to an unemployed undergraduate with modest academic credentials and no collateral.

Risks are also taken that involve institutional resources. Overcommitment of program funds is an accepted practice, based on the aid administrator's best estimate of the percentage of students awarded who will enroll, maintain their eligibility, accept placement on a college work-study job, and earn the full amount of their award. To end the federal fiscal year with 100 percent utilization of all resources is the goal, as underutilization adversely affects allocations from the federal government in following years and overcommitment requires replacement of federal dollars with institutional funds. The effective administrator will manage to maintain his own integrity even though the results of his risk taking are not always positive.

Conclusion

Effective administration of student financial assistance programs at a college or university, like effective administration of other subsystems, requires continuous planning, feedback, and evaluation; open lines of communication; and an atmosphere of trust. There must be willingness to adapt to changes in the environment, courage to take risks when indicated, and ability to learn from the consequences. Understanding of the mission of the institution as it relates to the goals of student assistance and recognition of the unique responsibilities and contributions of other subsystems to that mission will build bridges of mutual support and encourage integration of all the subsystems into a coordinated system. Utilization of a theoretical approach to planning, such as open system theory, may be helpful to campus administrators of student financial assistance programs.

The open system theory provides a framework for the administration of financial aid programs on a college or university campus. The problems described in this chapter do not exhaust the problems that may be encountered, nor will the suggested framework always offer appropriate solutions. Unless there is mutual trust and a free flow of information within the institution, it is unlikely that the financial aid administrator will be effective regardless of the management system he employs. Effective management of student financial aid programs or of any student service presupposes honest administration and leadership of the highest integrity from the executive officers of the institution.

Open system theory will not make funds available to a financial aid administrator if those funds are not otherwise available. It may, however, make a case for his needs in light of the institution's mission. But if the mission of the institution is unclear or unstated, neither open system nor any other theory will be much help to the financial aid administrator.

References

Bell, E. "Administration Planning: Science or Art?" *Planning for Higher Education,* 1978, 7 (3).

Eble, K. E. *The Art of Administration: A Guide for Academic Administration.* San Francisco: Jossey-Bass, 1978.

El-Khawas, E. *Management of Student Aid: A Guide for Presidents.* Washington, D.C.: American Council on Education, 1979.

Gaff, S., and others (Eds.). *Professional Development: A Guide to Resources.* New York: A Change Publication, 1978.

Garlock, J. "A Descriptive Survey of Directors of Financial Aid at Senior Institutions in Five Southwestern States." Unpublished doctoral dissertation, East Texas State University, 1980.

National Association of Student Financial Aid Administrators. *Characteristics and Attitudes of the Financial Aid Administrator: A Report on the Survey of the Profession in 1977.* Washington, D.C.: National Association of Student Financial Aid Administrators, 1978.

Parish, H.C. "Professional Associations—Genesis and Development." In R. Keene, F. C. Adams, and J. E. King (Eds.), *Money, Marbles, and Chalk: Student Financial Support in Higher Education.* Carbondale: Southern Illinois University Press, 1975.

Shirley F. Binder is director of student financial aid and assistant vice-president for student affairs at the University of Texas at Austin.

Some concluding remarks are followed by references to bibliographies, dissertations and additional publications covering material that is pertinent to the subject of student financial aid.

Conclusion and Further Resources

Shirley F. Binder

In the seven chapters comprising this sourcebook, the major theme is a plea for more rational decision making on student financial assistance programs by legislators and bureaucrats, and suggestions for institutional response to these changes that have been made are offered. Both Dallas Martin and Joe McCormick point out that the dollar volume available through the federal student assistance programs is significant not only to individual students but to the institutions in which they choose to enroll. In point of fact, institutions that face potential enrollment declines are beginning to recognize the importance of access, a term that has been central in the development of student aid programs. Access is now being addressed in the broader sense of facilitating entry and retention of students into the institutions of their choice, through a simple and coordinated process involving admissions, financial aid, housing orientation, and academic advising.

The attention of institutional executive officers has been focused on financial aid by the Office of Education, through the agreement to participate in Title IV programs, through a personal correspondence campaign, and through regional seminars designed specifically for presidents. The membership associations housed at One Dupont Circle in Washington, D.C. representing institutions by type and control have recently placed emphasis on dissemination to institutional presidents of information on the impact exerted by financial aid programs on institutions. One focus of attention for business officers and internal auditors through their professional associations has been financial aid. An understandable interest in the amount and kind of assistance that is made available to students as well as in the processes used to convey that assistance at the institutional level continues to be expressed by admissions officers and their associations.

The availability of financial assistance and knowledge of program eligibility and procedures are pertinent to the issues of student access and persistence. Sam Howell offers a model for institutional compliance with the spirit as well as the letter of student consumer regulations. Of equal importance to students are coordination of student services on campus and support for those services from top administrative levels. As pointed out by Jesús Gómez and Bob Treviño-Martínez, bridge building between the various campus services and reaching out to students to provide services rather than waiting for them to seek those services after failure will be necessary for institutional success, and in some cases for institutional survival, during the 1980s.

The results of computerization on an institutional aid office described by Gordon Allen and Jim Zimmerman can help an institution to facilitate student access. However, as they make plain, successful mechanization depends on a well-thought-out system that has the support both of the administration and of the staff. Decisions made during system development relative to financial aid programs affect both the organizational structure of the aid office and other student support services. Such decisions cannot be made in isolation, nor can they be imposed on a financial aid office by a central data processing office within the institutional structure or by an outside vendor. Mechanization must be supported by a system approach to the management of student aid functions. Shirley Binder has suggested the open system described by Edwin Bell as a possible model for financial aid office management. More important than a specific model, perhaps, is a resolve on the part of the aid administrator to utilize systems theory in management of aid programs.

In summary, we return to the major theme of this sourcebook: a plea for more rational decision making on student financial assistance programs, which will utilize such a model as that presented by Bill Van Dusen for research involving all the partners in the financial assistance programs: federal and state governments, institutions, and private donors. Certainly, we are all grateful that rising costs have not priced access to postsecondary education out of the reach of low- and middle-income students. However, we are not certain of the effect of heavy borrowing on students who choose to attend the high-priced institutions, nor can we predict the long-range effect on institutions that divert money from faculty salaries or facility renovation to scholarships for students. The cost of administering financial aid programs is only partly offset by the administrative allowance available to institutions participating in the campus-based federal financial assistance programs. Does the remaining cost represent the cost of doing business or is it more realistically described as the cost of compliance with federal regulations?

Obviously, the questions raised in these chapters far outnumber the answers. An awareness of the questions about the effect on students, their families, and institutions provoked by changes in federal student assistance programs is imperative for university presidents, student personnel service administrators, and students of higher education administration. Student financial aid administration is a growing, increasingly technical and specialized field, involving student services, fiscal affairs, and the academic community. It is an extremely visible service, and in the light of institutional budgetary considerations, its existence is highly defensible. For further material on the subject, the reader is directed to two excellent annotated bibliographies:

Henry, J. B. (Ed.). *New Directions for Institutional Research: The Impact of Student Financial Aid on Institutions,* no. 25. San Francisco: Jossey-Bass, 1980.

This sourcebook provides a good overview of the impact of student financial aid on institutions and their students. It also contains some practical suggestions for effective administration of such programs by institutions. The annotated references are quite inclusive.

Davis, J. S., and Van Dusen, W. D. *Guide to the Literature of Student Financial Aid.* New York: College Entrance Examination Board, 1978.

This is a very complete annotated bibliography of the resources on student financial aid published through 1977. The material is organized into seven major categories, and each category is prefaced by a description of the subject that allows the reader to find items of interest.

All dissertations on student financial aid are listed in two volumes of *The Journal of Student Financial Aid:*

"The Dissertation Corner." *The Journal of Student Financial Aid,* 1980, *10* (1), 43-51.
This issue contains the titles of all relevant dissertations completed between 1970 and 1979.

"The Dissertation Corner." *The Journal of Student Financial Aid,* 1980, *10* (2), 38-43.
This issue contains the titles of all relevant dissertations completed prior to 1970.

Two additional sources not listed in the annotated bibliographies described above are suggested to the reader.

Foxley, C. H. (Ed.). *New Directions for Student Services: Applying Management Techniques,* no. 9. San Francisco: Jossey-Bass, 1980.
The dearth of literature concerning management as it relates to education makes this volume, edited by a woman who teaches student services administration, extremely valuable for those preparing to enter the field.

Gladieux, L. E., and Wolanin, T. R. *Congress and the Colleges.* Lexington, Mass.: Lexington Books, 1976.
This volume, which describes the steps leading up to the enactment of the Education Amendments of 1972, treats the reader to a view of the strategies involved in the passage of a piece of omnibus legislation.

Shirley F. Binder is director of student financial aid and assistant vice president for student affairs at the University of Texas at Austin.

Index

A

Allen, G. E., viii, 69-82, 96
Allocation: analysis of, 11-24; application process in, 12-14; characteristics of process for, 15-16; conditional guarantees in, 17-18, 19-21; funding definitions in, 19; funding formula in, 18-19; funding results of, 21-23; goals for, 16-17; by institutional type, 21-22; modifications in, for 1980-81, 19-21; new process for, 16-19; old method of, 13-16; by state, 22-23; state allotment formulas in, 14-15, 17
American Council on Education, 33
Aulepp, L., 54, 66
Axt, R. G., 3, 10

B

Basic Educational Opportunity Grant, viii
Bell, E., 85, 86, 87, 88, 89, 90, 91, 92, 96
Bennis, W., 84
Binder, S. F., vii-ix, 83-98
Brockett, D., 10
Brown, W. F., 53, 54, 63, 66
Buchanan, T. M., 70, 82
Buffa, E. S., 72, 82
Bureau of Student Financial Assistance, 7, 22n, 23

C

California, campus-based aid allotments to, 23
Carnegie Council on Policy Studies in Higher Education, 69, 82
Center for Helping Organizations Improve in Education (Project CHOICE), 40
Chapman, D., 39, 40, 47
College Scholarship Service (CSS), 38, 40, 47, 54, 66
College Work-Study (CWS) program, 27, 29, 44, 86; allocation process for, 11-24; and peer counseling, 50, 53, 59
Computers: alternatives to, 77-81; benefits and drawbacks of, 70-71; for financial aid operations, 69-82; and systems concept, 72; trade-offs with, 72-76
Congressional Budget Office, 9
Conrad, C., 11, 24
Constitution, education in, 1-2
Consumer information. *See* Information, consumer
Cosand, J., 11, 24

D

Davis, J., 26, 34, 97
Delworth, U., 54, 66
Dewar, R., 73, 82

E

Eble, K. E., 88, 92
Education Amendments of 1976, 50, 53, 66
El-Khawas, E. H., 38, 47, 84, 92
Equal Opportunities Act of 1974, 56, 66

F

Federal government: allocation process of, 11-24; analysis of policies of, 1-10, and consumer information, 11-42; control by, 1-3, and evaluation results, 7-8; higher education policy of, 11; and information needs, 6-7; policy changes by, 6; regulatory impact of, 51-52; scope of education interests of, 3-4; and special interest groups, 8-9; specialized programs of, 3-5
Financial aid: administration of, 83-85; allocation process for, 11-24; amount of, 5, 11, 25, 69; computerized opera-

Financial aid *(continued)*
tions for, 69–82; consumer information on, 37–47; federal policies on, 1–10; and government regulations, 51–52; growth of, 69–70; history of, 50–51; importance of, vii; issues in, 95–97; open system theory for, 83–93; peer counselors for, 49–67; purpose of, 52; researching, 25–35; resources on, 97–98; technology in, effects of, 72–73, 75
Flippo, E. B., 73, 82
Ford, J. D., 75, 82
Foxley, C. H., 98
Frambs, G., 52, 66
Freeman, R. B., 34
Fund for the Improvement of Postsecondary Education (FIPSE), 40

G

Gaff, S., 84, 92
Garlock, J., 84, 92
General Accounting Office (GAO), 9, 12
Gladieux, L. E., 8, 10, 98
Gómez, J. R., viii, 49–67, 96

H

Hage, J., 73, 82
Halo error, concept of, 73–74
Halstead, C. P., 38, 43, 47
Henderson, C., 33, 34
Henry, J. B., 97
Higher Education Act of 1965, 4, 13, 16, 50
Howell, S., viii, 37–47, 96
Hoy, J. C., 38, 47
Huff, R., 12, 13, 16, 24, 30

I

Information, consumer: administrative allowance for, 37, 39, 41, 47; analysis of, 37–47; documents for, 41–42; draft outline for, 45–46; federal government and, 41–42; importance of, 39–40; institutional resources for, 43–45; kinds needed, 38; quality of, 39–40; review and research for, 43; system design for, 42–46

J

Jefferson, T., 4
Jepsen, K. J., 70, 82
John, L. G., 38, 47
Johnson, L. B., 4
Johnson, R. W., 52, 66

K

Kansas, campus-based aid allotments to, 23
Knight, G. A., 38, 47
Krejcie, R. W., 28, 34

L

Library of Congress, 9
Lloyd-Jones, E. M., 33, 34

M

McCormick, J. L., vii–ix, 11–24, 95
McGrath, E., 11
McKenzie, D., 54–55, 66
Martin, A. D., Jr., vii, 1–10, 95
Massachusetts, campus-based aid allotments to, 23
Michigan, University of, systems development at, 79–81, 82
Michigan Student Financial Aid Association (MSFAA), 70–71, 82
Middle Income Student Assistance Act (MISAA) of 1978, 5, 51
Midwest Association of Student Financial Aid Administrators, 31, 34
Morgan, D. W., 28, 34

N

National Association of Student Financial Aid Administrators (NASFAA), 26, 34, 83, 89, 92
National Center for Education Statistics, 15, 53, 54, 66
National Defense Education Act of 1959, 25
National Direct Student Loan (NDSL), 6–7; allocation process for, 11–24
National Student Educational Fund (NSEF), 53, 66
National Task Force for Better Information for Student Choice, 40

National Task Force on Student Aid Problems, 32, 34
Nelson, J. A., 27, 29, 35
New York, campus-based aid allotments to, 23
Northwest Ordinance of 1787, 2

O

O'Hearne, J. J., 25, 35
O'Keefe, M., 4-5, 10
Olson, L., 44, 47, 53, 54, 66
Open systems theory, concepts of, 85-91
Oregon, campus-based aid allotments to, 23

P

Parish, H. C., 83, 92
Peer counselors: analysis of, 49-67; evaluation of, 64-65; funding for, 59; objectives for, 57-59; for probationary students, 55-65; recruitment and selection of, 62-63; roles and responsibilities of, 59-61; supervision of, 61-62; training of, 63-64; use of, 53-55, 57
Peña, R., 55, 66
Pennsylvania, campus-based aid allotments to, 23
Pernal, M., 52, 66, 78, 82
Plummer, J. C., 33, 34

R

Research on financial aid: approach to, 25-35; basic questions in, 28-29; beginning, 27-30; lack of, 26-27; management of, 31-32; reasons for, 32-34; resources for, 29-30
Rodgers, W., 72, 82

S

Sanders, L. E., 29-30, 35
Schotten, P., 38, 47
Simon, H. A., 6, 10
Slocum, J. W., Jr., 75, 82
Smith, M. R., 33, 34
Southern Association of Student Financial Aid Administrators, 39, 42, 47

Stark, J. S., 38, 39, 40, 42, 43, 47
State governments, control by, 2-3
Stegura, D., 44, 47, 53, 54, 66
Students: consumer information for, 37-47; as consumers, 38-39; as peer counselors, 49-67; responsibilities of, 65-66; satisfactory progress of, 55-56; on scholastic probation, 49-67; support services for, 56-57
Supplemental Educational Opportunity Grant (SEOG) program, allocation process for, 11-24

T

Technology, effects of, 72-73, 75
Tennessee, campus-based aid allotments to, 23
Texas, University of, at Austin: computer use at, 76; Student Facilitator Program at, 55-65
Tiedt, S. W., 4, 10
Title IV legislation, 85, 95; and allocation process, 17; and consumer information, 39, 41
Treviño-Martínez, R., viii, 49-67, 96
Truman, H. S., 11

U

U.S. Department of Education, 24
U.S. Department of Health, Education, and Welfare (DHEW), 15, 46, 47, 50, 51, 66
U.S. Office of Education (USOE), vii, 6-7, 13, 14, 16, 22, 25, 38, 39, 47, 50, 53, 87, 95

V

Van Dusen, W. D., viii, 25-35, 50, 67, 97
Vaughn, G. B., 38, 47
Vejil, E., 55, 66

W

Washington, campus-based aid allotments to, 23
Wedemeyer, R. H., 71, 81, 82
Wisconsin, campus-based aid allotments to, 23
Wolanin, T. R., 8, 10, 98
Woodward, J., 72, 82

Y

Young, D. P., 38, 47

Z

Zimmerman, J. E., viii, 69-82, 96

New Directions Quarterly Sourcebooks

New Directions for Student Services is one of several distinct series of quarterly sourcebooks published by Jossey-Bass. The sourcebooks in each series are designed to serve both as *convenient compendiums* of the latest knowledge and practical experience on their topics and as *long-life reference tools*.

One-year, four-sourcebook subscriptions for each series cost $18 for individuals (when paid by personal check) and $30 for institutions, libraries, and agencies. Single copies of earlier sourcebooks are available at $6.95 each *prepaid* (or $7.95 each when *billed*).

A complete listing is given below of current and past sourcebooks in the *New Directions for Student Services* series. The titles and editors-in-chief of the other series are also listed. To subscribe, or to receive further information, write: New Directions Subscriptions, Jossey-Bass Inc., Publishers, 433 California Street, San Francisco, California 94104.

New Directions for Student Services
Ursula Delworth and Gary R. Hanson, Editors-in-Chief
1978: 1. *Evaluating Program Effectiveness,* Gary R. Hanson
      2. *Training Competent Staff,* Ursula Delworth
      3. *Reducing the Dropout Rate,* Lee Noel
      4. *Applying New Developmental Findings,* Lee Knefelkamp, Carole Widick, Clyde A. Parker
1979: 5. *Consulting on Campus,* M. Kathryn Hamilton, Charles J. Meade
      6. *Utilizing Futures Research,* Frederick R. Brodzinski
      7. *Establishing Effective Programs,* Margaret J. Barr, Lou Ann Keating
      8. *Redesigning Campus Environments,* Lois Huebner
1980: 9. *Applying Management Techniques,* Cecelia H. Foxley
     10. *Serving Handicapped Students,* Hazel Z. Sprandel, Marlin R. Schmidt
     11. *Providing Student Services for the Adult Learner,* Arthur Shriberg

New Directions for Child Development
William Damon, Editor-in-Chief

New Directions for College Learning Assistance
Kurt V. Lauridsen, Editor-in-Chief

New Directions for Community Colleges
Arthur M. Cohen, Editor-in-Chief
Florence B. Brawer, Associate Editor

New Directions for Continuing Education
Alan B. Knox, Editor-in-Chief

New Directions for Exceptional Children
James J. Gallagher, Editor-in-Chief

New Directions for Experiential Learning
Pamela J. Tate, Editor-in-Chief
Morris T. Keeton, Consulting Editor

New Directions for Higher Education
JB Lon Hefferlin, Editor-in-Chief

New Directions for Institutional Advancement
A. Westley Rowland, Editor-in-Chief

New Directions for Institutional Research
Marvin W. Peterson, Editor-in-Chief

New Directions for Mental Health Services
H. Richard Lamb, Editor-in-Chief

New Directions for Methodology of Social and Behavioral Science
Donald W. Fiske, Editor-in-Chief

New Directions for Program Evaluation
Scarvia B. Anderson, Editor-in-Chief

New Directions for Teaching and Learning
Kenneth E. Eble and John Noonan, Editors-in-Chief

New Directions for Testing and Measurement
William B. Schrader, Editor-in-Chief

274081

STATEMENT OF OWNERSHIP, MANAGEMENT, AND CIRCULATION
(Required by 39 U.S.C. 3685)

1. Title of Publication: New Directions for Student Services. A. Publication number: USPS 449-070. 2. Date of filing: September 29, 1980. 3. Frequency of issue: quarterly. A. Number of issues published annually: four. B. Annual subscription price: $30 institutions; $18 individuals. 4. Location of known office of publication: 433 California Street, San Francisco (San Francisco County), California 94104. 5. Location of the headquarters or general business offices of the publishers: 433 California Street, San Francisco (San Francisco County), California 94104. 6. Names and addresses of publisher, editor, and managing editor: publisher—Jossey-Bass Inc., Publishers, 433 California Street, San Francisco, California 94104; editor—Ursula Delworth, Gary R. Hanson, University of Iowa, Counseling Center, Iowa City, Iowa 52242; managing editor—JB Lon Hefferlin, 433 California Street, San Francisco, California 94104. 7. Owner: Jossey-Bass Inc., Publishers, 433 California Street, San Francisco, California 94104. 8. Known bondholders, mortgages, and other security holders owning or holding 1 percent or more of total amount of bonds, mortgages, or other securities: same as No. 7. 10. Extent and nature of circulation: (Note: first number indicates the average number of copies of each issue during the preceding twelve months; the second number indicates the actual number of copies published nearest to filing date.) A. Total number of copies printed (net press run): 2559, 2551. B. Paid circulation, 1) Sales through dealers and carriers, street vendors, and counter sales: 85, 40. 2) Mail subscriptions: 1116, 599. C. Total paid circulation: 1201, 639. D. Free distribution by mail, carrier, or other means (samples, complimentary, and other free copies): 125, 125. E. Total distribution (sum of C and D): 1326, 764. F. Copies not distributed, 1) Office use, left over, unaccounted, spoiled after printing: 1233, 1787. 2) Returns from news agents: 0, 0. G. Total (sum of E, F1, and 2—should equal net press run shown in A): 2559, 2551.

I certify that the statements made by me above are correct and complete.

JOHN R. WARD
Vice-President

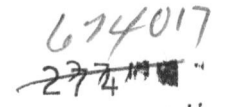